THE
HUMAN BODY

GET UNDER THE SKIN
WITH SCIENCE ACTIVITIES FOR KIDS

Kathleen M. Reilly

Illustrated by Alexis Cornell

More titles in the **Build It Yourself** Series

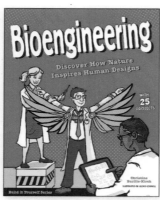

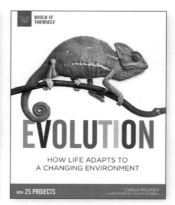

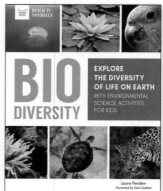

Check out more titles at www.nomadpress.net

Nomad Press
A division of Nomad Communications
10 9 8 7 6 5 4 3 2 1

This book was manufactured by CGB Printers,
North Mankato, Minnesota, United States
June 2019, Job #268929

ISBN Softcover: 978-1-61930-801-5
ISBN Hardcover: 978-1-61930-798-8

Educational Consultant, Marla Conn

Questions regarding the ordering of this book should be addressed to
Nomad Press
2456 Christian St.
White River Junction, VT 05001
www.nomadpress.net

Contents

Interested in Primary Sources?

Look for this icon. Use a smartphone or tablet app to scan the QR code and explore more! Photos are also primary sources because a photograph takes a picture at the moment something happens.

You can find a list of URLs on the Resources page. If the QR code doesn't work, try searching the internet with the Keyword Prompts to find other helpful sources.   🔎 human body

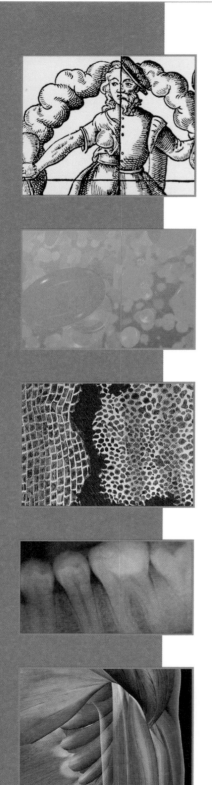

3000 BCE–300 BCE: The ancient Egyptians are the earliest people known to maintain accurate health records.

1700 BCE–220 CE: The ancient Chinese begin to search for medical reasons for illnesses.

1200 BCE–200 BCE: The ancient Greeks begin practicing modern medical science by observing the human body and the effects of disease.

460 BCE: Hippocrates, the "Father of Medicine," is born.

1506 CE: Leonardo da Vinci uses dissection to accurately draw the human body, both the outside of the human body and the inside of the human body.

1628: William Harvey describes the circulation of blood to and from the heart.

1796: Edward Jenner develops a vaccine for smallpox.

1865: Gregory Mendel publishes the results of his heredity experiment.

1879: The first vaccine for cholera is developed.

1881: The first vaccines for anthrax and rabies are developed.

1895: Wilhelm Conrad Röntgen discovers X-rays, which enable scientists to view the interior of the body without waiting until the body is deceased and can be dissected.

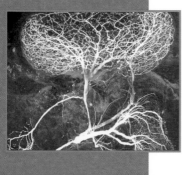

1896: The first vaccine for typhoid fever is developed.

1910: Marie Curie isolates radium, furthering the field of radiology, which eventually leads to new treatments for many different types of diseases.

1922: Insulin is first used to treat diabetes, granting a much-extended life to sufferers of the disease.

1928: Sir Alexander Fleming discovers penicillin, which leads to the development of a whole group of medications that treat bacterial infections.

1945: The first influenza vaccine is developed. Do you get a flu shot every year?

1952: Jonas Salk develops the polio vaccine.

1980: The World Health Organization announces that smallpox is eradicated through the use of vaccines.

2003: Scientists announce they have completed a draft sequencing of all the genes that make up human DNA.

2017: Gene therapy is used to cure a teenage boy with sickle cell disease.

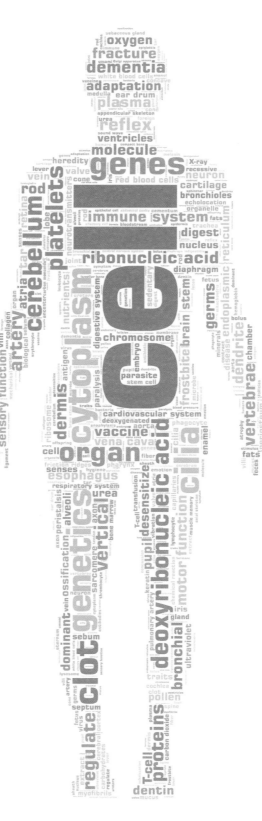

TAKE A LOOK!

When you look in the mirror, you see the same "you" who's always looking back. It's easy to go through your day sleeping, eating, walking, talking, doing homework—all without thinking about it too much. But under your skin, you've got an amazing set of systems that are working together to create the life you live.

Did you know you've got a river inside of you? You do, sort of—your bloodstream! Just as a real river carries boats up and down the waterways to their destinations, so does your **bloodstream**, shuttling **oxygen** and waste products all around your body.

ESSENTIAL QUESTION

Why are all of the systems of the body important? How does our body let us do what we want and keep us alive?

And you've got a furnace system, too. Your body can **regulate** its own temperature, cooling you down or warming you up. You stay the perfect temperature to keep all your systems on "go."

1

WORDS TO KNOW

bloodstream: the blood moving through the body of a person or animal.

oxygen: a gas in the air that animals and humans need to breathe to stay alive.

regulate: to control or to keep steady.

lever: a bar resting on a pivot used to lift and move objects.

joint: the point where two bones meet and move relative to one another.

X-ray: a photograph taken by using X-rays, a wavelength that can penetrate a solid.

humors: the fluids that people used to believe were responsible for the health of the human body. These included black bile, phlegm, blood, and yellow bile.

organism: any living thing.

cell: the basic unit or part of a living thing.

germs: harmful microorganisms, which are organisms that are too small to be seen with a microscope.

This is how we look under the skin!

You also have **levers** in the form of bones and **joints** and a highly developed computer system called the brain—all tucked into your skin in a neat order!

Have you ever thought about how it all works?

DISCOVERING THE BODY

Before there were **X-rays** and other machines that offered a glimpse inside a live body, doctors and scientists had to make some guesses about how things worked inside of us. One popular theory from ancient times was that evil spirits made you sick. Perhaps you offended a demon and, therefore, were struck down with the flu.

Later, people believed that the body was ruled by four different **humors**, or fluids, that had to be kept in balance. If you had too much bile in your body, for example, you'd get cancer.

Ancient doctors didn't have the knowledge that modern doctors do. However, in their studies and writings, they laid the groundwork for the doctors and scientists who came after them to develop an understanding about the human body.

As time passed, doctors and scientists began to realize there were tiny things that make up the human body and every other **organism**. They learned that our bodies consist of billions of **cells**. They also came to realize that **germs** can be spread through the air and by touch and that the simple act of washing hands goes a long way in stopping the spread of illness!

An illustration in a book from 1574 shows representations of the four humors people thought ruled the body.

All By Myself

Some parts of your body you can control, such as your movement or your speech. These are voluntary actions. Other parts of your body function all by themselves, without you having to think about them at all. These are involuntary. Do you think about your heart pumping blood? Do you have to tell your body to digest your dinner? Your body even works when you're sleeping! Your lungs keep sucking in air and releasing waste, your heart is beating, and your brain is even giving you something to dream about during the night!

WORDS TO KNOW

chamber: an enclosed space. The human heart has four chambers.

muscle memory: the way your muscles remember how to work.

extract: to take out.

deoxyribonucleic acid (DNA): the substance that carries your genetic information, the "blueprint" of who you are.

genes: sections of DNA that code for a particular trait, such as brown eyes and black hair.

It's amazing to think that we're walking, talking, and thinking because of the way trillions of cells are arranged. Together these cells create and protect the human body.

Each one of those cells is doing a specific job, forming your skin, creating new blood cells, or something else!

In *The Human Body*, we'll take a journey under your skin to learn how it really works. You'll create models that imitate your body's functions, and test some of those functions, too. You can take a peek inside a real heart to understand how yours is shaped and how the **chambers** work together to pump your blood. You can test your **muscle memory** and even **extract** the **deoxyribonucleic acid (DNA)** that carries your **genes** that make you who you are.

After reading this book, you might have a completely different reaction the next time you look in the mirror. That same "you" that looked so familiar before will now look like an amazing masterpiece—a living, breathing, thinking, feeling machine that is an example of the amazing human body.

Good Science Practices

Every good scientist keeps a science journal! Scientists use the scientific method to keep their experiments organized. Choose a notebook to use as your science journal. As you read through this book and do the activities, keep track of your observations and record each step in a scientific method worksheet, like the one shown here.

Question: What are we trying to find out? What problem are we trying to solve?
Research: What is already known about the problem?
Hypothesis/Prediction: What do we think the answer will be?
Equipment: What supplies are we using?
Method: What procedure are we following?
Results: What happened? Why?

Each chapter of this book begins with an essential question to help guide your exploration of the human body. Keep the question in your mind as you read the chapter. At the end of each chapter, use your science journal to record your thoughts and answers.

ESSENTIAL QUESTION

Why are all of the systems of the body important? How does our body let us do what we want and keep us alive?

TEST YOUR OWN REACTIONS

Your brain performs faster than you can even realize. Sometimes, your brain works all by itself—as in reflex reactions. Test your reflexes and see how you can teach your brain to react faster to a stimulus.

▶ **Place some masking tape along a ruler.** Divide it into six equal portions, measuring it and marking it with lines. Number each segment.

▶ **Get a friend to help.** Your friend will hold the ruler **vertically** with one hand by the upper edge with the number one position at the bottom. Position the fingers of one of your hands at the bottom of the ruler, below the number one position. You shouldn't be touching the ruler, just have your hand ready.

▶ **Ask your friend to let go of the ruler suddenly, without warning you.** Your job is to try to "pinch" or catch the ruler as it slips between your fingers, before it hits the floor.

▶ **Note the number where you caught the ruler.** This is your starting point, without any training.

▶ **Repeat the experiment several times.** See how fast you can get at catching the ruler. At what number can you catch it?

Try This!

As your brain begins to figure out how fast the ruler will fall, it sends a message to your fingers more and more quickly. This should improve your time every time the ruler is dropped. Try performing this experiment with your eyes closed. Can you rely on your **senses** to tell you when the ruler drops?

WORDS TO KNOW

reflex: an involuntary and often instantaneous movement in response to a stimulus.

stimulus: a change in an organism's environment that causes an action, activity, or response.

vertical: straight up and down.

senses: seeing, hearing, smelling, touching, and tasting. These are ways that people and animals get information about the world around them.

Chapter 1

THE
CARDIOVASCULAR SYSTEM

Would you believe a river of life runs through your body? It's your blood! Without it, your cells couldn't function at all.

Place two fingers lightly on the inside of your wrist. Do you feel that tiny thump that happens over and over again? That's your pulse. Your pulse measures the beat of your heart as it pumps blood throughout your body. That blood makes everything you do possible. Breathing, running, thinking—it all relies on your blood!

The path your blood takes as it moves through your body is called the **cardiovascular system**. And pumping steadily at the center of the cardiovascular system is your heart.

ESSENTIAL QUESTION

What job does blood play in keeping your body healthy and functioning properly?

WORDS TO KNOW

cardiovascular system: the body system that includes the heart and blood vessels. Also called the circulatory system.

nutrients: substances that organisms need to live and grow.

hormone: a chemical that travels through the bloodstream to signal other cells to do their job in the body.

carbon dioxide: the gas that's produced as a waste product by your body.

vein: a blood vessel that carries blood to the heart.

artery: a blood vessel that carries blood from the heart to the rest of the body.

capillaries: tiny blood vessels that connect the smallest arteries with the smallest veins and deliver oxygen and nutrients to the body's tissues.

plasma: the liquid part of blood.

red blood cells: cells that carry oxygen to all the cells of the body.

white blood cells: cells that protect against infection by destroying diseased cells and germs.

platelets: cells that help the blood clot, which helps stop a cut from bleeding.

proteins: nutrients that are essential to the growth and repair of cells in the body.

minerals: nutrients found in rocks and soil that keep plants and animals healthy and growing. Salt and nitrogen are two minerals.

In cartoons, the heart is usually shaped like a box of chocolates on Valentine's Day. But it's really shaped more like a fist— and it's about the size of a fist, too. Your heart's job is to push blood through the cardiovascular system, transporting blood everywhere from the top of your scalp all the way down to your little pinkie toe.

The heart is the superstar of the cardiovascular system, but your blood is amazing, too.

Blood makes up about 7 percent of your body weight! It carries oxygen, sugar and other **nutrients**, **hormones**, and vitamins to all parts of your body. At the same time, it helps get rid of waste products such as **carbon dioxide**. Blood also helps regulate your body temperature and keeps cuts from bleeding too much.

Blood travels through a maze of tubes called **veins**, **arteries**, and **capillaries**. These blood vessels all work together so your blood can do its job—which is to keep you healthy and strong!

You know that blood is the red stuff in your body. But there's a lot more to blood than its redness. Blood is made up of **plasma**, **red blood cells**, **white blood cells**, and **platelets**. Each has its own part to play.

PLASMA

Just a little more than half of your blood is made up of plasma. Plasma is about 92 percent water. The rest of it consists of **proteins**, dissolved salts, nutrients, and **minerals**. These float around in the plasma as it transports them where they need to go. Without plasma, your blood cells wouldn't be able to move through your body.

DID YOU KNOW?

When blood is donated, it is separated into its parts. Blood in a tube is spun around extremely fast. The force of the spinning separates the different types of cells into layers.

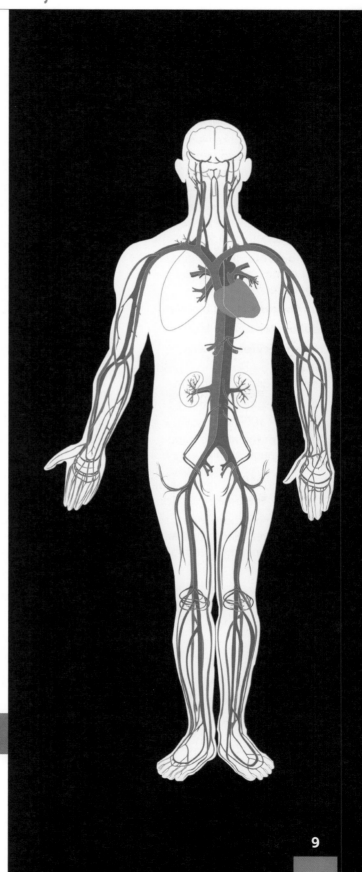

The cardiovascular system

bone marrow: spongy tissue inside some of your bones that contains stem cells.

stem cell: a self-renewing cell that divides to create cells with the potential to become specialized cells.

molecule: a group of atoms, which are the smallest particles, bound together to form matter.

hemoglobin: the protein that carries oxygen in your bloodstream.

erythrocyte: a red blood cell.

leukocyte: a white blood cell.

thrombocyte: a platelet.

disease: a sickness that produces specific signs or symptoms.

foreign: something that's not natural to your body.

infection: the invasion and multiplication of microorganisms, such as bacteria and viruses that are not normally present within the body, that make you sick.

bacteria: microorganisms found in soil, water, plants, and animals that are sometimes harmful but often helpful.

parasite: an organism that feeds on and lives in another organism.

RED BLOOD CELLS

Blood cells are produced in the **bone marrow**, which is a soft, spongy-like substance inside bones. Inside the bone marrow are **stem cells**. These cells constantly divide to make new blood cells to replace those that wear out. They speed up this production when necessary. For example, if the oxygen level in your body is too low, your kidneys will produce a hormone. This hormone "tells" the stem cells to start turning into red blood cells. After the stem cells turn into blood cells, they move into your bloodstream through the capillaries that run through your bones.

Red blood cells give blood its red color. They look like flattened doughnuts with the hole filled in. One drop of your blood contains millions of red blood cells. They don't live very long—only about 120 days—which is why you need so many new ones.

Red blood cells carry oxygen to other cells. First, they travel to the lungs to get oxygen. Once there, **molecules** inside the red blood cells called **hemoglobin** grab onto the oxygen. Then, when the red blood cells travel to a part of your body where the oxygen is low, the hemoglobin releases the oxygen for the cells to use.

What's in a Name?

Although it's easy to call the different parts of your blood by their simple names—red blood cells or platelets, for example— they also have scientific names.

Red blood cells: **erythrocytes**

White blood cells: **leukocytes**

Platelets: **thrombocytes**

DID YOU KNOW?

Some white blood cells are called "killer cells." Their job is to hunt down and destroy any other cells that are harming your body—such as cells that cause **disease** or your own infected cells.

WHITE BLOOD CELLS

White blood cells are bigger than red blood cells, and your blood has fewer of them. Even so, one drop of blood carries thousands of them.

White blood cells protect your body against foreign invaders.

Whenever an **infection** enters your body, the white blood cells find the harmful germs and work to destroy them. Different kinds of white blood cells attack different types of infections. Some battle **bacteria**, others take on **parasites**, and still others spring into action in the event of an allergic reaction.

White blood cells are created in the bone marrow, just like red blood cells. They also have a short life—from half a day to a few weeks.

Antoni van Leeuwenhoek (1632–1723) is credited as the first person to discover red blood cells. He wrote a letter describing his observations in 1675. **Three years later, Jan Swammerdam (1637–1680) drew the first known depictions of these cells.** **Take a look!**

PS

🔍 discovery red blood cells Virginia

PLATELETS

Platelets are another thing found in your blood. They are even smaller than red blood cells. Their job is to close off torn and cut blood vessels to stop the bleeding. They keep your blood where it belongs—inside you!

WORDS TO KNOW

clot: the clump of blood proteins and cells that forms over a cut to help stop the blood flow.

transfusion: the transfer of blood from one person to another.

immune system: the system that protects the body against disease and infection. Includes white blood cells.

antibodies: proteins that help the immune system fight infections or bacteria.

Platelets help make **clots** and scabs. When you cut yourself, the platelets gather up around the wound. They plug the wound so that it stops bleeding. After the bleeding stops, platelets create long threads made from a protein called fibrin. These fibrin threads stitch together and form a mesh over your cut. This is the clot. Red and white blood cells pile up behind this mesh and, before you know it, you've got yourself a scab. The scab protects the wound until the skin completely repairs itself. Try not to pick at it!

DID YOU KNOW?

Platelets got their name because of the way they look—like a disc made of two little plates stuck together! When they're in action, though, they change shape and look like they have tentacles.

Some wounds are deep enough that they need a little help in healing. That's when you might head to the doctor to get stitches.

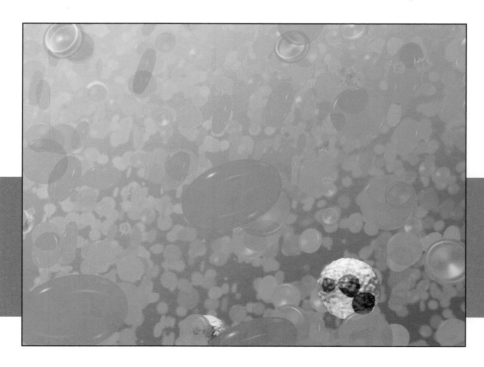

An illustration of red blood cells, white blood cells (white with dark shapes inside), and platelets (spiky red shapes)

The Life of a Blood Cell

› Blood cells are created in bone marrow—the stuff that's inside your bones.

› Newly made blood cells leave the marrow through blood vessels going through the bone and into the surrounding tissue.

› Blood cells spend their lives transporting oxygen, defending against invaders, and helping to clot and close wounds.

› Blood cells are short-lived—some kinds live half-a-day, others live for a few months.

BLOOD TYPES

Not everyone's blood is the same. Your red blood cells may carry a different protein on them than your friend's blood cells. The protein that rides on the blood cells identifies the four main blood types—A, B, AB, and O. Blood type A has A-type proteins, type B has B-type proteins, type AB has both kinds of proteins, and type O has neither.

Your blood type matters if you're ever in need of a **transfusion**. If a person with type A blood receives type B blood, their body will think the B proteins are invaders, and their **immune system** will produce **antibodies** against it. However, a person with type AB blood can receive either type A or type B blood. And anyone can receive type O blood, because it has neither of the offending A or B proteins. But someone with type O blood can receive only type O blood.

Where does all of this blood come from for transfusions? Many people are able to donate blood, which gets tested and sorted and stored so that when it's needed, it's ready.

WORDS TO KNOW

aorta: the large artery carrying blood from the heart.

vena cava: the main vein carrying blood into the heart.

valve: a structure that controls the passage of fluid through a tube, such as blood through veins.

blood pressure: the pressure of the blood against the inner walls of the blood vessels.

tissue: a large number of cells similar in form and function that are grouped together, such as muscle tissue or skin tissue.

YOUR INNER ROADMAP: VEINS, ARTERIES, AND CAPILLARIES

Your blood moves through your body in blood vessels called arteries, veins, and capillaries. These flexible tubes branch out like tree limbs, getting thinner as they reach the outer points of your body.

Arteries carry blood away from the heart to the rest of the body. Veins carry blood back to the heart.

The main artery from the heart is called the **aorta**. The main vein into the heart is called the **vena cava**. Arteries and veins are similar in that the walls of both are made of three layers. They have a strong outer layer, then a muscle layer, and finally a sleek, inner layer that allows the blood to flow easily.

Arteries and veins are very different, too. The walls of veins aren't as thick as walls of arteries, either. And there's another difference—because the heart is pushing the blood out through your arteries, the blood is flowing in one direction—away from your heart. But with your veins, the blood is on a return trip from your body, and your heart isn't pushing blood through them with the same force.

DID YOU KNOW?

Capillaries are very tiny but can be different sizes. The capillaries in your ears, for example, are much finer than the arteries coming directly out of your heart.

Veins use **valves** along the way to keep the blood moving in the right direction—toward the heart. Even if you're upside down, your veins will keep moving blood toward your heart.

Blood Pressure

Your blood is pumped through your blood vessels with a certain force by your heart. The amount of that force is called your **blood pressure**. Having good blood pressure is important because if it's too high—because of smoking, poor nutrition, or not exercising enough—you're making your heart work harder than is healthy for it. And you really want to keep your heart ticking as well as possible for a long time to come!

Blood pressure is measured by figuring out how well blood squeezes through a restricting band in a certain amount of time. This is why a blood pressure "cuff" is put around your arm to measure your blood pressure.

Capillaries are tiny with very thin walls. They're so narrow that blood cells line up, single-file, to travel through them. While veins and arteries transport the blood around your body, the capillaries are the tubes responsible for getting oxygen and nutrients into your body **tissues**. The thin capillary walls allow oxygen and nutrients to pass through them to reach your body's cells.

AT THE HEART OF IT ALL

The heart, like your veins and arteries, has three layers in its wall, all with big names. "Cardio" is part of all three words because cardio comes from the Greek word for heart—*kardia*. The outer layer is called the pericardium. The next muscle layer is called the myocardium, and the smooth, inner layer is called the endocardium.

WORDS TO KNOW

atria: the chambers of the heart that receive blood from the veins.

ventricles: the chambers in the heart from where blood is forced into arteries.

deoxygenated: without oxygen.

oxygenated: filled with oxygen.

septum: a thick layer of muscle between the two sides of the heart that keeps blood separated.

contract: to squeeze or force together.

Although similar in shape to a fist, the heart is not a solid block of muscle. It contains four hollow chambers. In the top half of your heart are the left and right **atria**. In the lower half of your heart are the left and right **ventricles**.

So what path does blood take through your heart? Blood with little or no oxygen, called **deoxygenated** blood, arrives from the rest of your body into the right side of your heart through your right atrium. Then, it's pumped to the ventricle on your right side, before being pumped to your lungs to pick up oxygen. At the same time, another batch of blood returning from your lungs, called **oxygenated** blood, arrives in the atrium and ventricle on the left side of your heart, and the strong left ventricle then pumps it out to your body.

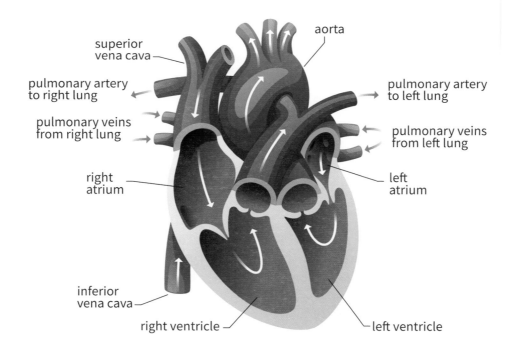

Heart valve

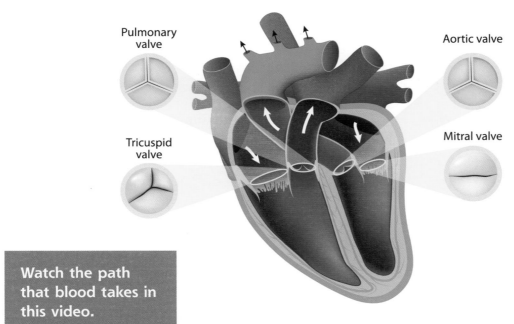

Pulmonary valve

Aortic valve

Tricuspid valve

Mitral valve

Watch the path that blood takes in this video.

PS

🔍 Kahn circulatory system

Between each atrium and ventricle is the valve that keeps the blood moving in the proper direction through the heart. Also, a thick layer of muscle between both sides of your heart, called the **septum**, keeps the blood separated. These chambers all work together in a steady rhythm to move deoxygenated blood to the lungs and oxygenated blood from the lungs to the rest of the body.

Your heart beats because of an electrical impulse that causes its muscle to **contract**. Each heartbeat has two stages. In the first stage, the left and right atria contract, moving blood into the left and right ventricles. In the second stage, the ventricles squeeze, pushing blood out of the heart. During a small pause as the muscle relaxes, the heart fills up with blood again, ready for the next heartbeat.

DID YOU KNOW?

The blood returning through your veins to your heart has so little oxygen that it's bluish in color. That's why you can see blue veins on the inside of your wrist.

mitosis: the process of cell division.

membrane: the outer layer. The membrane of a cell allows materials to pass in and out.

cytoplasm: the jelly-like fluid inside a cell.

organ: a part of the body with a special function, such as the heart, lungs, brain, and skin.

organelle: a structure within a cell that has a special function.

AND WHAT ABOUT CELLS?

We've already mentioned cells a lot in this chapter. For example, you've seen how blood cells move around your body. But what is a cell?

Cells are the smallest living things in your body. They're sometimes called the body's "building blocks." Scientists aren't sure how many cells are in your body, but estimates range between 50 to 100 trillion! And keep in mind that the cells in your body change constantly as old cells die and new ones are created.

All living things have cells, though plant cells are a bit different than human and animal cells. But all of our cells have the same basic job—to maintain the human body and care for it at a cellular level. Non-living things don't have cells—you're not going to find a cell in a rock or your shoe.

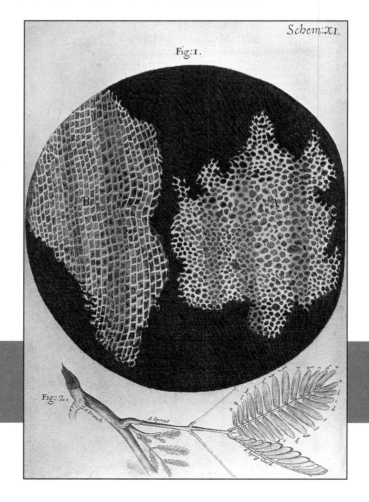

A drawing of cells from a cork tree, by Robert Hooke, who first identified them, 1665

credit: Wellcome Collection (CC BY 4.0)

Cells work hard to get energy from food, provide fuel to other cells, clean up dead cells, gobble up invading germs, and even reproduce themselves. They're pretty busy, bustling around inside of you like a microscopic city hard at work every day.

Cells can make copies of themselves. The copies are called "daughter" cells. Each daughter cell is an exact replica of the original "mother" cell. Through a process called **mitosis**, cells divide to reproduce themselves. Without mitosis, your body wouldn't be able to create all the new cells it needs when the old ones wear out.

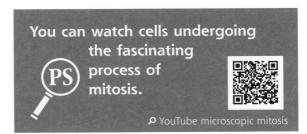

You can watch cells undergoing the fascinating process of mitosis.

PS

YouTube microscopic mitosis

YOUR CELLS: A CLOSE-UP LOOK

If you want to look at a cell from your body, you'll need a microscope. The first thing you might notice about a cell is that it has a border around it. That's the cell **membrane**. It holds everything inside the cell.

But your cell membrane is not quite solid. Materials can move in and out—but only if the guards let them through. That's right, your cell membrane contains proteins that act as guards. If something belongs in the cell, the guard proteins let it enter.

The cell itself is filled with a gooey, jelly-like substance called **cytoplasm**. What is this stuff? Well, just as your body has **organs**—your heart and stomach, for example—your cells have tiny parts that function as their organs. They are called **organelles**, meaning "tiny organs."

DID YOU KNOW?

Cells got their name because, under a microscope, they look like little rooms, or cells.

WORDS TO KNOW

nucleus: the part of a cell that holds your genetic information.

ribonucleic acid (RNA): genetic material that contains the code to make a certain protein.

mitochondria: organelles within a cell that produce energy.

endoplasmic reticulum: a network of membranes that makes changes and transports materials through a cell.

Golgi apparatus: a cell organelle that tags molecules for specific areas inside or outside a cell.

ribosome: the protein-making factory in a cell.

lysosome: a cell organelle that contains digestive enzymes that break down waste material.

enzyme: a substance that causes chemical reactions to occur.

chemical reaction: the process when two or more molecules interact and change.

Here are a few of the organelles that can be found in different kinds of cells.

Nucleus. Inside each cell is a nucleus, the control center that holds all the genetic information about you. This information is contained in microscopic strands of material called deoxyribonucleic acid (DNA) and **ribonucleic acid (RNA)**.

Mitochondria. Sometimes called "mighty mitochondria," these submarine-shaped organelles are the powerhouses that produce most of the energy your cells need to live and perform their functions.

Endoplasmic reticulum. This tongue-twister name is appropriate for this organelle—it's shaped like a stack of envelopes. Its job is to move proteins around a cell.

Golgi apparatus. The Golgi apparatus—which looks like a stack of bent pancakes—packages up proteins and sends them to the cell membrane. From there, the proteins pass through to the environment outside that cell, to be used as your body needs them.

See what many of these organelles look like under a microscope. What do you think it was like for the scientists who first examined them?

🔎 Dr Jastrow organelles

Ribosomes. Tiny little spheres called ribosomes make protein.

Lysosomes. These organelles are responsible for cell cleanup. Armed with **enzymes**, lysosomes use the **chemical reactions** enzymes cause to break down old organelles or invading germs to remove them from the cell.

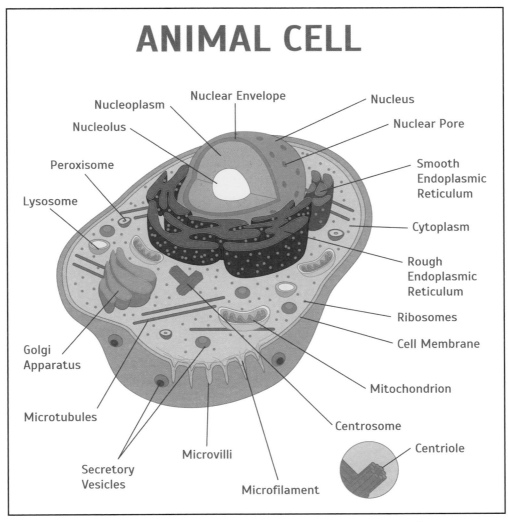

ANIMAL CELL

Nucleoplasm
Nuclear Envelope
Nucleus
Nucleolus
Nuclear Pore
Peroxisome
Smooth Endoplasmic Reticulum
Lysosome
Cytoplasm
Rough Endoplasmic Reticulum
Ribosomes
Cell Membrane
Golgi Apparatus
Mitochondrion
Microtubules
Centrosome
Centriole
Microvilli
Secretory Vesicles
Microfilament

If you see an organelle you don't recognize, do some research!
Head to the library or look it up online and find out what that organelle does.

WORDS TO KNOW

melanin: a brown pigment in skin.

epithelial cell: a type of cell found on the surfaces of the body and the organs that acts as a protective barrier.

Different scientists discovered each of the organelles at different times. Meet some organelle explorers!

• In 1833, Robert Brown discovered the nucleus.

• The mighty mitochondria were first observed by Albert von Kolliker in 1857. These were named "mitochondria" by Carl Benda in 1898.

• The Golgi apparatus was discovered in 1898 by Camillo Golgi.

• Albert Claude and Keith Porter identified the endoplasmic reticulum in 1945.

• Ribosomes were discovered in 1955 by George Palade.

Cells and blood are two things that all living things need! In the next chapter, we'll take a look at another crucial system in your body: The respiratory system!

ESSENTIAL QUESTION

What job does blood play in keeping your body healthy and functioning properly?

Special Jobs, Special Cells

Your body has more than 200 different kinds of cells! Each kind has a specific job to do, so it might need a special shape or feature to do that job effectively.

> **Blood cells.** You've already learned that you have red and white blood cells and platelets, all performing different jobs in your blood stream.

> **Melanin cells.** These cells are in your skin. **Melanin** is responsible for producing skin color that protects the skin from damaging rays in sunlight.

> **Muscle cells.** These long cells contract forcefully, usually to cause movement.

> **Skin cells.** Cells called **epithelial cells** are layered to form the outside layer of your skin. We'll learn more about skin cells in Chapter 5.

MAKE YOUR OWN EDIBLE CELL

Of course, you need a microscope to see actual cells and their organelles. But with this activity, you can create a much larger—and more delicious!— version to study.

Caution: An adult must help you with the boiling water.

❯ **Pour two 8-ounce packages of lemon powdered gelatin** (or another flavor with a pale color) into a large bowl. Stir in 2½ cups boiling water. Be sure to mix it for at least 3 minutes to make certain the gelatin is completely dissolved.

❯ **Spray a plastic cup with nonstick cooking spray** and fill it halfway with gelatin. Put it in the refrigerator to chill.

❯ **When the gelatin is firm, take your cup out of the refrigerator.** Push a gumball in the center of the gelatin (to represent the cell's nucleus). Then, use candy to make the rest of the organelles in the cell: round cake sprinkles (ribosomes), red fruit leather (endoplasmic reticulum), green fruit leather (Golgi bodies), and hot tamales (mitochondria).

❯ **Make another batch of gelatin** and, while it's still liquid, pour it very slowly into the cup. If you pour down the side of the cup, you'll get better results.

❯ **Carefully return the cup to the refrigerator until the gelatin is firm.**

❯ **When the gelatin is set, carefully slide the cell out of the cup.** If you're having trouble, try sliding a butter knife around the edges. If the cup is disposable, just peel it away.

❯ **Examine your cell before eating it**—you should be able to see all the organelles inside! How would making a model help scientists do research?

Think About It!

How would our bodies function differently if it weren't for some of these very specific organelles and the work that they do?

PUMPING HEART SQUIRTER

Do you want to see the chambers of your heart in action? With this pump system, you can see how blood flows from the atria to the ventricles, and how it's pumped under pressure out to your body. When you're ready to get it pumping, though, head outside—this project will definitely get your surroundings wet!

▶ **Take the caps off four small plastic drink bottles.** Poke holes in the caps large enough for a straw or plastic tubing.

▶ **Snip a drinking straw or plastic tubing into two pieces, each about 3 inches long.** Thread one piece of straw (or plastic tubing) through two of the caps. Do this for both straws. Put a binder clip on each piece of straw, pinching it shut. You'll have two sets of two caps connected with one straw. Use modeling clay to plug any space around the holes in the caps where the straws went in.

▶ **Get four more tubes or straws.** If you're using plastic tubing, cut two very long pieces—about 10 inches or longer. If you're using straws, push one inside another until you have a very long straw. Be sure you don't crunch the tip of the straw too much when you push it inside the other, or you won't have a good "blood" flow. Tape the straws together gently. Do this twice, so you end up with two very long tubes.

▶ **Cut a hole in the bottom of two of the bottles.** These will be your atria. You're going to be pouring water in through these holes.

DID YOU KNOW?

When you were first born, your heart beat around 140 times per minute! But as an adult, it beats only half that fast.

> **In the other two bottles, poke a hole in the top sides** (near the "shoulder" of the bottles). These will be your ventricles. Thread your long straws or tubing through these side holes, pushing the straws all the way to the bottom of the bottles. Use modeling clay to plug around the holes in the bottles where the straws enter.

> **Screw all four caps on the bottles.** Be sure your atria are at the top and upside down, with the holes at the top. Tape both the atria together with electrical tape, and tape both ventricles together. The tubes from the ventricles will rise up past the atria, so you may want to gently tape them against the atria so they're not flopping around.

> **Dye a batch of water red for oxygenated blood.** Pour it into one top bottle (atrium). Dye another batch of water blue (for deoxygenated blood) and pour it into the second atrium bottle. The binder clips will keep most of the water from moving on to the ventricle bottles—just like the valves in your heart keep the blood from moving on to the next chamber.

> **Go outside and, when you're ready, release the water by removing the binder clips.** The water will flow into the ventricles. Close the valves by replacing the binder clips.

> **For the second part of the heartbeat, squeeze the bottom bottles.** The "blood" will shoot out of your straws or tubing through pressure!

Try This!

Sometimes, when people have heart disease, it's because one or more of their ventricles are partially blocked. You can simulate this by putting a small ball of modeling clay in one or both of your tubes. How hard is it to get the blood flow going now?

Chapter 2

THE RESPIRATORY SYSTEM

Take a deep breath—now blow it out! Breathing is an automatic action for most people, so we don't spend a lot of time thinking about it. But without breathing, we wouldn't be doing much of anything else!

Every day, you breathe in and out without thinking about it—even when you're sleeping. That's because your **respiratory system** is doing its job. It brings air into your lungs so your cells can get the oxygen they need. Your lungs aren't the only things working in the respiratory system, though. Your nose, **trachea**, and **bronchial** tubes all pitch in, too. Let's take a look at all the different parts of the respiratory system.

ESSENTIAL QUESTION

How do your lungs supply oxygen to your body?

LUNGS

Along with the heart, the lungs are the key organs in our chest. Their job is to breathe in oxygen and breathe out carbon dioxide. Unlike your heart, your lungs aren't made of muscle. They consist of stretchy, spongy tissue that expands and contracts as you inhale and exhale.

Your left lung shares space with your heart and has two **lobes**, or sections. Your right lung has three lobes. The lobes all work the same way. And although your lungs are squishy and could be easily damaged, the bony cage of your ribs protects them from any harm—and protects your heart, too.

When you breathe in, you pull air into your body—but it's not just a straight shot to your lungs from your nose or mouth. Inside your lungs, it's very moist. Bacteria and viruses love moisture, and could easily create an infection in your lungs. That's why it's important for the outside air (which may be carrying unwanted guests) to pass through a series of defenses, or a series of filters, before it reaches your lungs.

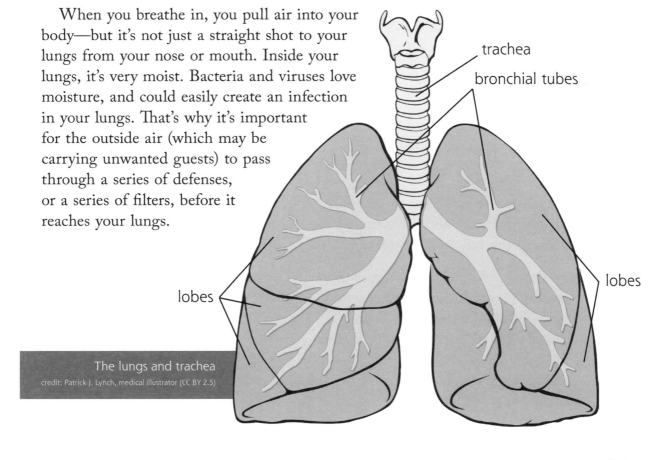

trachea

bronchial tubes

lobes

lobes

The lungs and trachea
credit: Patrick J. Lynch, medical illustrator (CC BY 2.5)

WORDS TO KNOW

cilia: tiny "hairs" that line your nose and trachea.

mucus: slimy, sticky substance that lines the nose.

cartilage: stiff, flexible tissue that mostly converts to bone in adults.

diaphragm: the muscle that separates the chest from the abdomen.

THE NOSE KNOWS

Air first enters your body through your nose. Of course, your nose is for smelling, but it's also an important part of your respiratory system. For one thing, your nose warms the air that you're breathing to help bring it to body temperature.

Your nose is also lined with little hairs called **cilia** and sheets of sticky **mucus**. These catch tiny particles of dust and bacteria and prevent them from traveling to your lungs. If you've ever had a tickle in your nose and sneezed, it's probably because your nose was doing its job and getting rid of unwanted intruders.

DID YOU KNOW?

Even though you can breathe through your mouth, it's better to breathe through your nose. The mouth doesn't filter out particles in the air.

TRACK THE TRACHEA

You might be surprised to know that your nose is not just what you can see on your face. It's also a big cavity that lies above the roof of your mouth and goes all the way back to the top of your throat.

The air you breathe in travels from the nose and throat, through your larynx, or voice box, and then into your trachea. The trachea contains more mucus and cilia that help capture any particles that made it past your nose. Small rings of **cartilage** always keep your trachea open. If you gently push on the front of your lower neck you can feel the stiff rings. If any little particles get caught in your trachea, you automatically cough to get rid of them.

DIAPHRAGM

Your lungs aren't muscles, so they can't move themselves. (You'll learn more about muscles in Chapter 4.) When you breathe in and out, your chest rises and falls. But this isn't because your lungs are sucking in air on their own. That job belongs to two parts of your body that work together. These are the muscles of your chest wall and a dome of thin muscle at the bottom of your chest called the **diaphragm**.

When you breathe in, the chest muscles between your ribs and your diaphragm all contract. Lay your hands on your chest, take a deep breath, and feel your rib cage expand. This expansion of the chest cavity makes the air from outside your body rush in and inflate your lungs. When you breathe out, those same muscles relax, pushing the air back outside your body.

You breathe in oxygen, but you breathe out carbon dioxide. Just as blood comes to pick up oxygen in the lungs, it also drops off the waste created by cells there. So even though the air coming out of your nose feels the same as the air coming in, it's quite different.

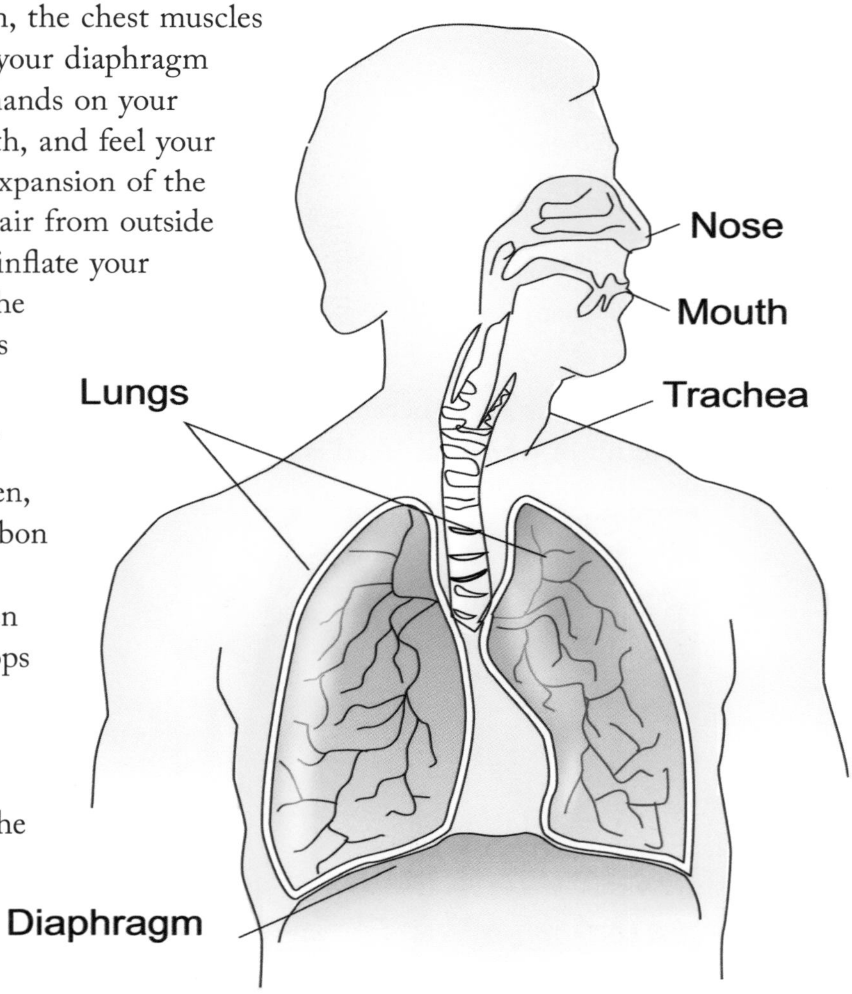

Nose

Mouth

Trachea

Lungs

Diaphragm

medulla: the part of the brain connected to the spinal cord that contains the centers controlling involuntary vital functions.

genetics: the study of genes and heredity. Genes are basic units in our cells that carry characteristics from one generation to the next.

carbon monoxide: a colorless, odorless, very toxic gas that is in cigarette smoke.

tar: brown, sticky substance found in cigarettes.

virus: a non-living microbe that can cause disease. It can only spread inside the living cells of an organism.

microbe: a tiny living or non-living thing. Another word for microorganism.

symptom: the sign of a disease, such as coughing or red bumps.

Your breathing is controlled by a part of your brain called the **medulla**. When you're running low on oxygen—or if your body suddenly needs more, for example, when you're exercising—your medulla increases the speed and depth of your breathing. Now, your body's cells get the oxygen they need.

WHEN THE BREATHING GETS TOUGH . . .

If all goes well, you'll probably breathe about 600 million times during your life. But sometimes, people have problems with their respiratory systems. Some problems come about because of lifestyle choices. Other problems occur because of something in the environment. Still others are a result of **genetics**. And some are medical mysteries.

A diaphragm in necessary to blow bubbles!

One lifestyle choice that leads to problems is smoking. As you saw, your body has defenses against intruders, such as the cilia and mucus lining your nose and trachea. But some things, including cigarette smoke, can overpower those defenses.

When people smoke, they're breathing in **carbon monoxide** and other dangerous chemicals. Cigarette smoke damages the cilia so they're not as effective against other intruders. Also, smoke carries a brown, sticky substance called **tar**, which can get stuck in the lungs and cause cancer. Because carbon monoxide gets picked up by the red blood cells, these cells can't hold as much oxygen and the heart must pump harder to supply more oxygen. Smoking has been shown to cause diseases such as emphysema and lung cancer.

Even smoking just one cigarette a day can lead to serious health complications.

Have you caught a cold yet this year? An example of something in the environment that causes problems with your respiratory system is the common cold **virus**. This **microbe** is left behind by another person when they have a cold and sneeze or cough. And it can give you a cold.

You're probably familiar with the **symptoms** of a cold: sneezing, coughing, stuffy or runny nose, and sore throat. One of the best defenses against catching a cold is to wash your hands often. This gets rid of the germs.

DID YOU KNOW?

Some scientists estimate that when you sneeze, the air blows out of your nose at around 100 miles per hour!

Cover your mouth when you sneeze!

WORDS TO KNOW

pollen: a fine, yellow powder produced by flowering plants. Pollen fertilizes the seeds of other plants as it gets spread around by the wind, birds, and insects.

esophagus: the long tube that connects your mouth to your stomach.

epiglottis: the flap of cartilage that covers the windpipe.

bronchioles: the tiny branches inside the lungs.

alveoli: the tiny air sacs in the lungs where the exchange of oxygen and carbon dioxide takes place.

pulmonary artery: an artery that carries poorly oxygenated blood from the right ventricle of the heart to the lungs.

DID YOU KNOW?

Your trachea and **esophagus**, or the tube that food travels down, are very close to one another. To keep food from going down your trachea, a little flap—called the **epiglottis**—covers your trachea and closes when you eat.

Allergic reactions can also bother your respiratory system. Allergies are usually due to something that's floating in the air, such as animal dander, dust mites, or **pollen**.

If you look at pollen under a microscope, you can see why it might be irritating to people's airways—it looks like sharp, bristly beach balls! When people are bothered by irritants such as this, their bodies often react with a sneezing fit or a runny nose.

Asthma is a more serious reaction to airborne irritants. When people with asthma breathe in irritating things, a chemical process causes their breathing passages to narrow and fill with mucus. This makes it very hard to breathe. People with asthma can inhale medication that works to open up the airways so that they can breathe more easily.

BRONCHIAL TUBES

Your trachea branches into two tunnels, called bronchial tubes. These go into your lungs and divide into smaller and smaller branches called **bronchioles**. Eventually, the bronchioles get so small that they're just tiny sacs of air.

These sacs of air in the lung are called **alveoli**. These are where the transfer of gases takes place in your lungs. When deoxygenated blood arrives in your heart, it's pumped through the **pulmonary artery** to each of your lungs. There, it dumps off carbon dioxide into the alveoli in your lungs and you breathe it out. When you breathe in, the oxygen in the air hitches a ride with the hemoglobin in the red blood cells. Then, that newly oxygenated blood heads back to the heart.

Now that you know how your body gets the oxygen it needs from the air you breathe, we'll take a look at how it gets the nutrients it needs from the food you eat!

ESSENTIAL QUESTION

How do your lungs supply oxygen to your body?

Hiccup!

Everyone has had hiccups at one time or another (and somehow it always seems to happen when you're supposed to be quiet!). When you hiccup, your diaphragm spasms on its own. You can't control it. According to scientists, many different things can cause hiccups—laughing too hard, eating spicy foods, or eating too quickly, for example.

A man named Charles Osborne (1894–1991) hiccupped for 68 years straight, earning him a spot in the *Guinness Book of World Records*. In an interview, Osborne claims to have begun hiccupping after a fall, which burst a small area of blood cells in his brain. **Read more about his life here.**

🔎 Charles Osborne hiccups

MAKE YOUR OWN MODEL LUNG

You've learned that lungs aren't muscles that move themselves. Instead, they depend on air pressure in your chest cavity and movement from your diaphragm and chest muscles to inflate and deflate. Here's how you can see this in action.

Caution: Have an adult help you poke the hole in the cap.

❯ **Cut the bottom off a 2-liter bottle.** Put a small balloon on the end of a straw and secure it with a rubber band. This is going to act as one of your lungs.

❯ **Poke a hole in the bottle cap and push the straw up through it** so the balloon hangs below. Use modeling clay around the top to seal where the straw comes out of the cap.

❯ **Cut the neck off a larger balloon and then stretch it over the bottom opening** of the bottle. Secure it in place with a rubber band. This balloon will work as your diaphragm.

❯ **Look at the small balloon (the lung).** It's hanging, empty, like your lungs before you breathe in. Then, gently pinch the diaphragm balloon to get a good grip and pull down slowly. The lung balloon fills with air. When you release the diaphragm balloon, the lung deflates.

What's Happening?

Your lungs fill with air because your diaphragm contracts and goes down, increasing the volume of your chest cavity. This decreases the air pressure inside you, and air is pulled in from the outside to fill the extra space—filling your lungs. When your diaphragm relaxes, that extra air must go somewhere, so it's forced back out of your lungs.

MAKE YOUR OWN MAGIC AIR BALL

Test your lung power and see how long you can keep a ball hovering over the end of a straw.

❯ **On the end of a straw nearest its bendable elbow, cut four small, evenly spaced slits.** They should be about ½-inch long from the tip to make four tabs at the end of the straw. Bend the tabs back at a right angle to the straw.

❯ **Bend the end of the straw up at its elbow.** The two parts of the straw will be at right angles to each other.

❯ **Bend one end of a pipe cleaner or thin wire into a halo shape.** About 2 inches down the pipe cleaner, tape the length of the pipe cleaner to the upturned straw. Try to position the halo about an inch above the opening in the straw. You can cut any excess pipe cleaner off the other end.

❯ **Place a lightweight ball on top of the halo and blow gently through the straw.** See how much lung power you must use to lift the ball. Then, try blowing continuously so the ball hovers over the halo. See if you can contract your breath to get the ball to come back down to its resting spot.

Think More!

How well do you think you could blow the ball if you had a chest cold?

Chapter 3

THE DIGESTIVE SYSTEM

Ever wonder why that apple you ate for lunch is better for your body than the slice of chocolate cake you had for dessert, or how your body processes any food at all? It's all thanks to your digestive system.

When you eat food, your body doesn't judge if it's "good" food or "bad" food. It just starts breaking down the food and figuring out how to get the most energy from it. This process of transforming the food into energy is called **digesting**. Everything you put into your body gets processed one way or another. Your digestive system not only breaks down food into its simplest nutrients, but it also absorbs these nutrients into your bloodstream.

ESSENTIAL QUESTION

Why are some foods better for your body than others?

It leaves the **indigestible** parts alone, to pass out of your body. If you eat more than your body needs and absorb more nutrients than your body can use, they get turned into fat.

LET'S GET THE PARTY STARTED

Your digestive system isn't all guts and innards. In fact, you can easily see one very important part of your digestive system—your teeth! When you bite, rip, and chew your food, you're starting the digestive process. With help from your tongue and saliva, all that chomping breaks down your food into smaller pieces. Smaller pieces make it easier for the rest of your system to extract the nutrients it needs from the food. So eat slowly, take small bites, and chew your food well!

First Bite

Have you ever swallowed something that was too big, and you felt that lump in your throat? Chewing your food enough is important. Your teeth are the first step in digestion, and your body would thank you not to forget that!

Here's how some teeth look in an X-ray.

Your tongue plays an important role in the digestive process, too. Although it looks like one flap of tissue, it's actually a group of muscles banded together. These muscles place food between the chewing teeth and then guide it to the back of your mouth to swallow.

WORDS TO KNOW

gland: an organ that makes and releases substances the body needs.

pharynx: the first part of your throat, right after your mouth.

bolus: the soft blob of chewed food that you swallow.

peristalsis: the squeezing process of moving food through your esophagus, stomach, and intestines.

abdominal cavity: the middle section of the body that holds organs including the stomach, liver, large intestine, and others.

sphincter: a round muscle that opens and closes to let something pass through.

Your teeth are designed to help you tackle all kinds of food.

Incisors are the teeth in the very front of your mouth. They are for shearing off pieces of food. Canines are the pointy ones in the front of your mouth. They are for tearing food. The flat teeth toward the rear of your mouth are your molars, and you use them for grinding and chewing food into smaller pieces.

You also have **glands** in your mouth that produce saliva. Saliva lubricates the food in your mouth so it's easier to chew. It also has chemicals in it that start breaking down the food. You have a large salivary gland in the back of your mouth and two smaller ones under your tongue.

After your teeth, tongue, and saliva break down your food, it passes through your throat, called the **pharynx**. Then, the food enters the esophagus—the muscular tube leading to your stomach.

What Happens When You "Lose Your Lunch?"

Nobody likes to throw up. But it's usually your body's way of protecting you against something, whether it's a bad piece of sushi or a virus. When you get sick, your stomach squeezes between your abdomen and your diaphragm, forcing the contents in your stomach to travel back up the way they came—out through your mouth (yuck!). What triggers this response can be anything from having too much food in your stomach, a stomach flu, or something poisonous in your body to feeling extremely scared or sad.

At this point, the blob of food is called a **bolus**. It's a roundish mass of food shaped from your chewing and stuck together with saliva. Its round shape is perfect to move it easily through your digestive system, and is part of the reason it's important to chew your food well!

As you swallow, the muscles of the pharynx act like a clenching hand to squeeze the bolus downward. Meanwhile, the epiglottis is folding over your larynx, preventing any food from going the wrong way, into your trachea.

Once the bolus is in the esophagus, the muscular wall of this tube moves it to your stomach by a series of rhythmic contractions. This process is called **peristalsis**.

The next stop is your stomach. This is a bean-shaped, hollow organ that's at the end of your esophagus. Although you may think your "belly" is your stomach, the stomach reaches a little higher up than you probably think. It's positioned on the upper left side of your **abdominal cavity**.

On top of the stomach is a ring of smooth muscle called a **sphincter**. This prevents the acidic stomach contents from squeezing up to burn your esophagus and throat. Another sphincter at the bottom of your stomach controls the food leaving the stomach and entering the small intestine.

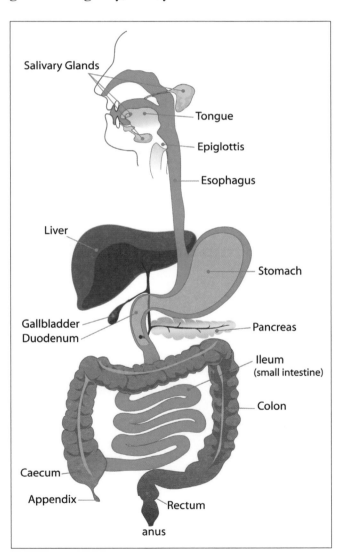

Your digestive system! Look up the parts of the system that are unfamiliar.

When the bolus lands in your stomach, your body gets to work breaking it down from something you'd recognize into chemical nutrients that your body uses for all its different functions. As your stomach muscles move the food around, acids split it apart and enzymes begin to break it down further.

After the stomach does its job, your food is a mushy liquid.

The contents of your stomach then move on to the small intestine. This organ is only a little more than 1 inch wide, which is why it's called the "small" intestine. However, it's about 20 feet long! In the small intestine, many enzymes come in from the nearby pancreas. These enzymes pummel the now-liquid food and are responsible for most of the digestion that takes place in the digestive system.

From Table to Toilet: How Long Does It Take?

After you swallow your food, how long does it take to go through the digestive process?

> In about half an hour, food reaches the stomach, where acids begin to break it down.

> Two hours after you eat, the food starts traveling down the long small intestine, where most food is broken down and most nutrients are absorbed.

> After about six hours, your stomach is empty again.

> After about 18 hours, wastes are starting to form in your large intestine. The water is absorbed by your body and any solid waste begins moving toward your rectum.

> After about 24 hours, the wastes are ready to leave your body.

Besides digesting, the small intestine absorbs the resulting nutrients into little fingers on its inner walls. The fingers are called **villi**, and they contain tiny capillaries that receive the nutrients.

After your food has made its long journey through the small intestine, it's still mushy, but your body has already absorbed much of the liquid and nutrients. What's left now enters the large intestine, which is about 3 inches wide and 5 feet long. It drapes around your abdominal cavity, running up one side, across the top, and down the other side. In the large intestine, more fluids are absorbed from what's left of the food, and helpful bacteria work on breaking down any tough food matter, such as **fiber**.

That's right—bacteria live inside your body! But how do we know this? Bacteria are microorganisms that are much too small to see with your eyes alone. Fortunately, Antoni Van Leeuwenhoek, who was mentioned in Chapter 1, invented a more powerful version of the microscope that allows us to see the tiny bacteria that help us break down the food we eat. **Watch a video about what his invention meant.**

🔍 Vox van Leeuwenhoek

WORDS TO KNOW

feces: poop.

urinary system: the organs concerned with the formation and discharge of urine.

urea: a waste product made from cells.

ureters: tubes connecting the bladder to the kidneys.

fats: one of the basic building blocks of nutrition and a rich source of energy.

carbohydrates: one of the basic building blocks of nutrition and a source of energy.

At this point, little liquid is left, and anything that remains—stuff your body just can't use for anything—is a soft solid waste, called **feces**. The last step for your now completely digested food is to move through your rectum. This is the end of your large intestine, where feces travel before being expelled out of your body through your anus.

DID YOU KNOW?

Even if you were upside down, your food would still move in the right direction down your esophagus toward your stomach. This is because of peristalsis.

URINARY SYSTEM

Solid waste is handled through your large intestine and rectum. Liquid waste is handled differently, because waste molecules are constantly produced by all the body's cells. These wastes enter your blood and are disposed of through the **urinary system**. One such waste product is called **urea**.

You have two kidneys, and their job is to filter out urea from your bloodstream. Kidneys are bean-shaped organs a bit bigger than a deck of cards. They're located near the middle of your back. Tiny kidney tubes filter and clean the blood while making your urine, which contains urea and all other waste products from the bloodstream. The urine then gets passed down to your bladder through tubes called **ureters**.

When the bladder is full, your brain receives a message from nerves in the stretched bladder wall that tells you it's time to go to the bathroom.

Other parts of your body play a role in the digestive system, even if food doesn't pass directly through them.

Your liver—the largest gland in your body—provides your digestive system with bile, a yellow-green substance that helps break down **fats**. Your liver is in the upper right portion of your abdominal cavity. The pancreas is just behind your stomach and secretes enzymes that help digestive juices break down protein and **carbohydrates**.

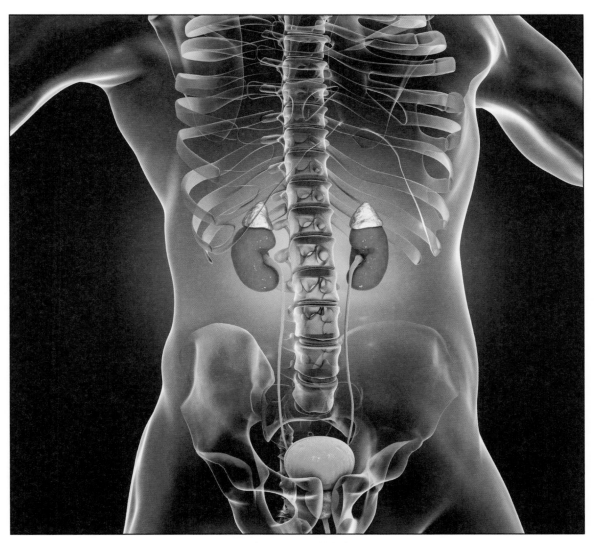

The kidneys and bladder

WHAT'S IN IT FOR ME?

Now that you know how your body breaks down food, just how does the body use what it has broken down?

Food is made of different kinds of nutrient molecules. When your digestive system breaks down food, it's reducing everything to its molecular level—through saliva, chewing, and each of the digestive organs. Along the way, your body pulls out the chemicals and molecules it needs and shuttles them off to be given to cells all around your body.

And that's what keeps your body healthy and functioning!

Part of a healthy body is one with muscles and bones that do the job of supporting and moving you. That's what we'll focus on in the next chapter.

ESSENTIAL QUESTION

Why are some foods better for your body than others?

NUTRIENT	WHAT THEY DO	FOUND IN
Carbohydrates	Main source of energy, sugars easily used by body	Bread, cereal, crackers, grains, fruit, starchy vegetables, dairy products
Proteins	Cell growth and repair, make hormones and enzymes	Meat, fish, tofu, beans, eggs, dairy products
Fats	Back-up energy, provide insulation	Dairy products, avocados, nuts, olive oil
Vitamins	Essential to body functioning, help immune system and battle disease	Fruits, vegetables, whole grains
Minerals	Necessary for body functioning	Lean meat, liver, some fish and nuts

Why do we need nutrients? Here's why!

MAKE YOUR OWN TOOTH CAST

Using your teeth to chew is one of the first steps in the digestive process. You see them in the mirror when you brush, but have you ever really taken a good look at them? This project will let you see what your teeth look like from all angles, and how they fit together to make a good chewing surface.

❯ **Use a moldable plastic mouth guard from a sports shop.** With an adult's help, follow the directions to boil and mold it to your teeth! Repeat this with both top and bottom teeth to make two casts. If you are doing this project with a friend, compare your casts and discover what's different and what's similar.

❯ **Cut some construction paper into two 2-inch strips.** Wrap the paper around the top edge of both molds. Make sure that at least 1½ inches of paper are above the edges. You'll be filling this with plaster of Paris, so it must be high enough so that the plaster won't spill over.

❯ **Mix together some plaster of Paris and water in a paper cup until you have a thick consistency.** Pour it into your molds. Tap the clay on the table a little to be sure you don't have any air pockets.

❯ **Wait until the plaster is dry**, then remove the paper and the clay. You'll have a perfect model of your teeth!

Try This!

See if you can identify the different types of teeth and what you use them for when eating. Can you spot any crooked teeth? Missing teeth?

BALANCE YOUR OWN NUTRITION

If you look at the food plate created by the U.S. Department of Agriculture, you can figure out how much of each food group is recommended for your size and age. But sometimes it's hard to keep track of what you've eaten and from which food group. Here's an easy way to keep track by balancing dried beans. Once you build this simple balance, just move beans from one side to the other. When the balance is even, you've eaten a balanced diet!

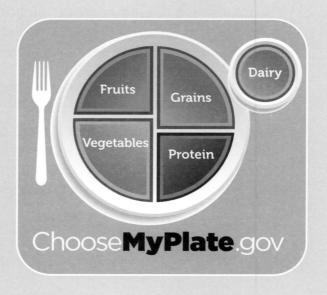

> To make your balance, straighten out a coat hanger. Cut it about a foot long, with the hook at one end. This is the base of your balance.

> Stick the unhooked end of the coat hanger into a foam block. You've now assembled the stand.

> Take another straight piece of coat hanger (about 10 inches long). Bend each end into a hook, then tie four pieces of string (each about 4 inches long) to each end.

> Poke four holes in one paper cup around the rim, then carefully tie one string into each hole. Repeat this with a second paper cup. These are the containers for your counting beans.

Activity

❯ **Balance the free piece of coat hanger from the hook on your balance stand.** You may have to slide it more to one side or the other until it's at the perfect spot to balance the empty cups. Once you have the right spot, stick a small piece of modeling clay on either side of the balancing wire so it won't slide one way or the other. If you're still having problems balancing, you can also add a small piece of modeling clay as a weight to one side or the other. Set the balance aside.

❯ **Count out 42 beans.** Paint five beans orange, seven beans yellow, three beans blue, and six beans red (or choose your own colors, but keep the number of beans the same as listed here). You'll have 21 unpainted beans—these are your balance beans.

❯ **When the paint is dry, put all 42 beans in one cup.** You're now ready to start keeping track.

❯ **Whenever you eat something during the day, move one of the beans to the second currently empty cup.** Here's how to choose the beans.

If you eat:

* a fruit or vegetable, move an orange bean.

* a grain, move a yellow bean.

* a dairy product, move a blue bean.

* a protein, move a red bean.

If you've eaten a balanced diet during the day, your scale will be balanced and you will have a very colorful collection of beans on the "eaten" side!

Think About It!

What would happen if you ate only foods from one food group all the time? How would that impact your body?

Chapter 4

MUSCLES
AND BONES

YOUR MUSCLES DO MORE THAN JUST HELP YOU MOVE.

THEY POWER YOUR WHOLE BODY!

REMEMBER THAT YOUR HEART IS A MUSCLE, TOO!

YOUR MUSCLES CAN BE WEAK OR STRONG.

EVEN YOUR BONES ARE CONTROLLED BY YOUR MUSCLES!

What moves the human body? Muscles, of course. Any movement you make—rolling your eyes at a bad joke, kicking the game-winning goal, even breathing while you sleep—it's all controlled by muscles.

Your muscles are also hard at work moving parts of your body you can't even see. As you already learned, muscles move food through your digestive system, make your heart beat, and pump blood through your body.

Your muscles are working hard, even if all you are doing is lying on the couch!

ESSENTIAL QUESTION

How do muscles help your body move?

When you think of a muscle, you might picture the bulge when you tighten your upper arm. But muscles come in all different shapes and sizes. They can be triangle-shaped, like the one in your shoulder that helps you raise and lower your arm. They can be flat and wide, such as abdominal muscles. And they can be ringed, such as those controlling the food coming in and out of your stomach.

DID YOU KNOW?

The smallest muscle and the smallest bone are found in the middle ear. The muscle is called the stapedius, and the bone is the stapes. They work together to help conduct sound through the ear so you can hear and to protect against loud sounds.

When babies are first born, they don't have much control over their movements. They have to train their brains to work together with their muscles. As you get older, you gain much more control over your muscles. Some people, such as athletes, dancers, or musicians, have such control over their muscles that they can perform amazing feats.

Imagine the muscles this person is using to do this move!

WORDS TO KNOW

myofibril: a cylinder of muscle protein made up of stacked sarcomeres. Myofibrils are the units of a muscle fiber.

sarcomere: a segment of contracting tissue that stacks to make up the myofibrils that, in turn, make up the muscle.

sheath: a protective cover for your muscles.

neurotransmitters: a brain chemical that carries information throughout the brain and body.

tendon: tissue that connects muscle to bone.

MUSCLE MAKEUP

If you could see the muscles under your skin, they'd look like groups of slick bands. These bands are muscle fibers and are made up of thin threads called **myofibrils**, which are themselves made of strands of protein called **sarcomeres**. Binding the whole muscle together is a tough cover called a **sheath**.

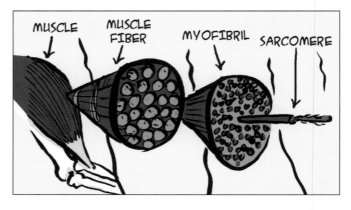

Your brain sends messages to your muscles by sending signals along your nerves. When a muscle receives these signals from your brain, its fibers contract and cause the body part attached to that muscle to move as well.

Your muscles never push body parts—they only pull. But they can move your body parts in a push-pull motion by working together. Think about throwing a ball. First, your biceps muscle on your upper arm pulls your forearm back to bring the ball up into throwing position. When you throw the ball forward, the muscle on the underside of your upper arm—your triceps—contracts, pulling your forearm down to complete the throw. The simple act of tossing a ball is actually quite complicated!

DID YOU KNOW?

When your muscles cramp—causing hard, painful lumps—it's because they contract and stay that way. You need to gently stretch them back out.

MAKING THEM MOVE

You have different kinds of muscles, but they all work in pretty much the same way. Some muscles are voluntary, meaning you choose to make them move—you decide to raise your hand or lift your foot to walk up a step. Other muscles are involuntary, meaning they move without you even thinking about it—such as your heart muscle pumping blood or your stomach digesting food.

Both kinds of muscle movements are controlled by your brain. The brain sends out signals through long nerve fibers, which then send the signals to your muscle fibers by chemicals called **neurotransmitters**. These tell the muscle fibers how much, how often, and when to contract. Now, let's look at different voluntary and involuntary muscles.

Skeletal. Your skeletal muscles are those that you can control. With these, you can move your arms, legs, mouth, and eyes whenever you like. Their fibers are the longest and thickest of all. If you were to look at your skeletal muscles under a microscope, they'd look like striped rods.

Skeletal muscles are usually attached to your bones—with tough connective tissue bands called **tendons**. But not all skeletal muscles are connected to your bones. The skeletal muscles on your face, for example, are attached to your skin. This lets you make different facial expressions by moving different parts of your face, such as your eyebrows and mouth.

atrophy: a decrease in size of a body part, such as a muscle.

Your skeletal muscles are strong, but they can get tired very quickly. If you squeeze your hand into a fist repeatedly, you'll very quickly tire your hand. That's unlike your cardiac muscle, or your heart, that pumps and pumps all day, every day without getting tired.

Smooth. You don't choose to move your smooth muscles—they move on their own. Smooth muscle is in the walls of your blood vessels and air tubes, as well as in the walls of your inner organs, such as your stomach, intestines, and bladder. For example, your stomach moves to pass food through it. You don't even have to think about it. Smooth muscles do their job, day after day, without you giving them a second thought.

If you looked at your smooth muscles under a microscope, you'd see they're not striped rods like skeletal muscles. Instead, they're pointed at the ends and bundled in flat sheets that look smooth. These muscles can contract for long periods without tiring out, unlike your skeletal muscles.

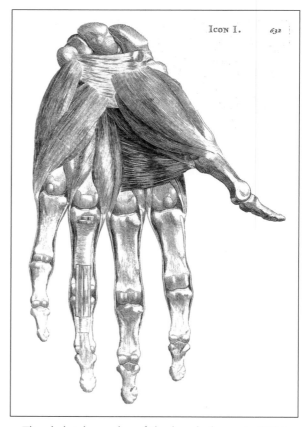

The skeletal muscles of the hand, drawn in 1734
Credit: Wellcome Collection (CC BY 4.0)

Cardiac. As you can probably guess from the name, the cardiac muscle is the one in the wall of your heart. Your cardiac muscle contracts constantly—it's what makes your heart beat. Under a microscope, your cardiac muscle cells look like striped, branched barrels.

MUSCLE MEMORY

DID YOU KNOW?

Some of the face muscles that are connected to the skin are a little shorter than others. So, when you smile or talk, the skin pulls in slightly—creating dimples! Dimples can fade as you grow older and the muscles stretch out.

When you learned how to walk, skip, throw a ball, or brush your teeth, you got better at it the more you did it. That's partly because your muscles were getting stronger as you grew. But it's also because of something called muscle memory.

As you repeat a movement over and over, your muscles begin to remember everything that happens. They remember exactly how hard to pull, when to stop pulling, and the angle they're pulling at. Of course, it's really your brain and spinal cord learning how to control and coordinate groups of muscles.

That's why you don't hit yourself in the head with your hairbrush every morning when you try to brush your hair. Your arm, hand, and head all remember just where to position themselves so you end up with a good hair day—not a bad headache.

GROW, BABY, GROW!

If you've seen people who work out all the time and push their muscles to the limit, you know that people can grow huge muscles. When you exercise, you can increase the size of your muscles or make them firmer. But did you ever wonder what would happen if you just lay in bed all day, every day? If you did this, your muscles would shrink, or **atrophy**—and you'd be really bored, too!

See a fun explanation on how muscles grow.

PS

Vimeo muscles grow

WORDS TO KNOW

sedentary: not moving around much.

Although the chance of you just lying around never lifting a single finger is pretty rare, it's still important to move your muscles a lot and keep them strong. Muscles grow stronger when you exercise, because every time you make your muscles work hard, some of the muscle fibers are damaged.

That's why your muscles ache if you do something you don't usually do, such as lift something heavy. The next day, your damaged muscle fibers are busy repairing. When those muscle fibers heal and regrow, the muscle becomes larger. When people work out very hard—lifting weights, for example—they intentionally damage their muscle fibers, then rest and let those fibers heal and build up. As they repeat the cycle, the fibers not only grow, but they also increase in number as they split and form new fibers.

DID YOU KNOW?

In 2007, a man named Zafar Gill lifted 136 pounds—with his ear! He used gym weights that hung from a clamp attached to his ear.

On the flip side, if someone doesn't use a muscle at all, it doesn't keep building new fibers and the muscle will atrophy, or become smaller and weaker. If you break your leg and have a cast on it all summer and can't run around, when the cast is removed, those leg muscles may look smaller than those on the other leg.

It takes a lot of training to lift heavy weights!
credit: U.S. Air Force

People who work at **sedentary** jobs, which can mean sitting at a desk all day, sometimes find they've lost muscle tone. Instead of being hard and firm, their muscles are a bit flabby and soft. But the cool thing about muscles is that you can always change them—just exercise!

WHAT ABOUT BONES?

If you pick up an earthworm and hold it by one end, what happens? It slumps right over and curls down along your fingers. Why? Because it doesn't have bones. The earthworm has no framework inside to hold it up. Without your skeleton, you, too, would be a slug-like mass of muscles and organs. You'd probably be able to move around, like the earthworm, but you wouldn't be able to stand upright and do all the things you're used to doing—such as running and jumping.

But the bones of your skeleton do a lot more than let you stand up and move around. They also make your blood cells and protect your organs from damage.

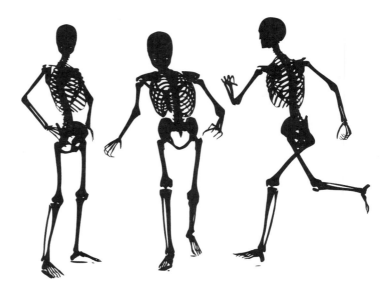

WORDS TO KNOW

axial skeleton: the ribs, backbone, skull, and sternum.

sternum: the wide, flat bone that joins your ribs together in front, also called the breastbone.

appendicular skeleton: arm and leg bones.

periosteum: the membrane on the outside of a bone.

compact bone: the white, hard, outer part of a bone.

ossification: the process of bone formation with the help of minerals such as calcium.

Scientists divide the human skeleton into two parts. The first part is called the **axial skeleton**. It is centered around the midline (axis) of the body and consists of your backbone, **sternum**, ribs, and skull. The axial skeleton protects organs such as your lungs, heart, and brain.

The second part of the human skeleton is called the **appendicular skeleton**. These are the bones in your limbs, such as your arm and leg bones. This part of the skeleton lets you move around and do everything from running and jumping to opening a jar of pickles.

Wave!

X-rays are electromagnetic waves of energy that make it possible to see bones through skin. The first X-ray ever taken was of the hand of the wife of the man who discovered X-rays, Wilhelm Conrad Röntgen (1845–1923).

credit: Wellcome Images (CC BY 4.0)

BONE CONSTRUCTION

When people die, the soft parts of their body decay. Only their bones are left behind. That's why the symbol for pirates or deadly chemicals is a skull and crossbones. But why do bones stick around so much longer than other body parts? It's because of what they're made of.

Bones have to be lightweight—so we can move around easily—but very strong. Adults' bones make up only 15 percent of their body weight, but ounce for ounce, they're stronger than steel! If you compared equal amounts of bone and steel, your bones would be stronger.

Your bones have layers. The outer membrane is a very thin but tough layer called the **periosteum**. The periosteum has blood vessels running through it that allow blood to enter the bone.

The next layer is **compact bone**. This is the hard, white stuff you think of when you imagine skeletons. But if your skeleton were made completely of compact bone, it would be too heavy. It's not too heavy because underneath the compact bone is a kind of network of thin pieces of bone. This is sometimes called "spongy bone" because of the way it looks.

Some bones have another part inside them, a soft tissue called bone marrow. And inside the bone marrow are special cells called stem cells. As you learned in Chapter 1, these cells give rise to all our blood cells.

Not Quite Bone

Your ears and nose aren't made of bone. They're made of cartilage, a tough connective tissue. When babies are developing, most of their bones are made of cartilage. As they grow, the cartilage turns into hard bones. This process is called **ossification**. But plenty of cartilage remains in our bodies. For example, it covers the ends of your bones at the movable joints and connects your ribs to your breastbone.

STRONG CHOMPERS

As strong as your bones are, your teeth are even stronger! Teeth are covered with **enamel**, the hardest stuff in the human body. But it's not indestructible, of course. Its weakness is sugar decay.

The sugars and natural bacteria in your mouth can break down the enamel. So, brush those teeth well!

Underneath the enamel is a yellow, bone-like material called dentin. If you have a cavity, it's usually because a hole in the enamel leaves the **dentin** exposed. At the center of your teeth is pulp. Pulp is the soft innards of your tooth containing important blood vessels and nerves. The nerves are the tooth's main message carriers to the brain.

The part of your teeth that's visible is called the crown. And your teeth are connected to your jaws by their roots. These are covered by a bony substance called **cementum**. Softer than dentin, cementum anchors fibers that hold the tooth in its socket.

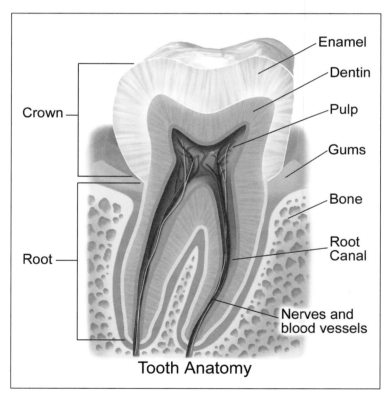

Tooth Anatomy

Crown — Root

Enamel — Dentin — Pulp — Gums — Bone — Root Canal — Nerves and blood vessels

credit: Blausen.com staff (2014); "Medical gallery of Blausen Medical 2014" (CC BY 3.0)

SHAPES AND SIZES OF BONES

When you think of bones, the first shape that may come to mind is a long bone with knobby ends. Some bones do look that way, of course. The long bones of your legs and arms look just like that. But other bones have different shapes, such as your skull, for instance. It's made of several plates joined together. And your two pelvic bones are wide and slightly **concave**, very different from any other bones in your body. There's a big range in size, too. Your femur, or thigh bone, is the largest. The smallest? The three tiny bones inside your inner ear.

The place where bones come together is called a joint. Joints help you move. The kind of movement that's possible depends on the joint. Different kinds of joints allow different kinds of movements.

Ball-and-socket joint. Examples of ball-and-socket joints are the joints that connect your arm to your shoulder and your leg to your hip. The bone of your arm or leg ends in a knob, or ball, that fits into the bowl-shaped socket of your shoulder or hip. This setup lets you rotate your arm or leg in different directions.

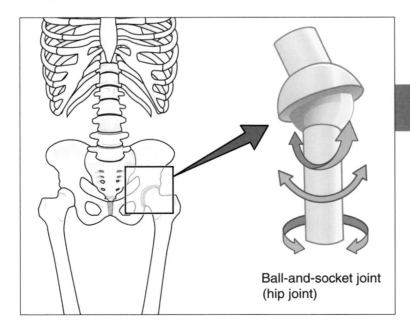

A ball-and socket joint
OpenStax College (CC BY 3.0)

Ball-and-socket joint
(hip joint)

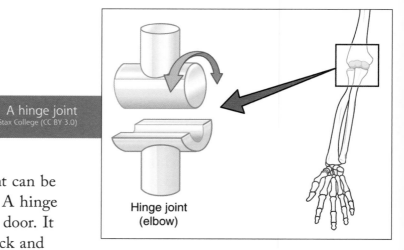

A hinge joint
OpenStax College (CC BY 3.0)

Hinge joint
(elbow)

Hinge joint. This kind of joint can be found at your elbows and knees. A hinge joint is similar to the hinge on a door. It lets you move your lower arm back and forth and your lower leg up or down. It's one-way only, though; it won't let you bend your arm or leg in the other direction.

Saddle joint. Where your thumb bone meets your hand bone is an example of a saddle joint. Picture a saddle, right-side up. Then picture a second saddle, upside down. If you laid the upside-down saddle on top of the first one, you'd get a saddle joint. This kind of joint allows you to move your thumb forward, backward, and side to side so you can grab onto things. It's not quite as flexible as the ball-and-socket joint, though.

Pivot. The backbone in your neck is an example of a pivot joint. This lets your head move from side to side smoothly.

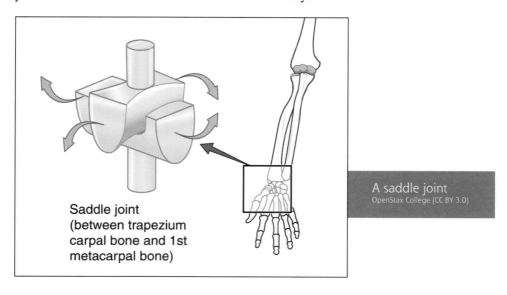

Saddle joint
(between trapezium
carpal bone and 1st
metacarpal bone)

A saddle joint
OpenStax College (CC BY 3.0)

STANDING UP STRAIGHT

Your backbone, or **spine**, is actually a chain of bones called **vertebrae**. Each vertebra looks slightly oval on the bottom with three "wings" behind. It also has a hole in the arch. This is where your spinal cord, the nerve cord that extends from your brain, runs. Your vertebrae protect your spinal cord and support your weight.

The vertebrae are divided into the following groups.

• **Cervical vertebrae.** These are the first seven bones in your spinal column. They are in your neck and support your head.

• **Thoracic vertebrae.** These are the next 12 vertebrae in your backbone. They're larger than cervical vertebrae, and each is connected to a rib.

• **Lumbar vertebrae.** The five lumbar vertebrae come next and are in your lower back. They're the largest of the vertebrae because their job is to support the weight of your body.

• **Sacrum.** Unlike the other vertebrae, the sacrum is triangular-shaped. It starts out as five vertebrae when you're born. As you get older, they fuse into a single bone. The sacrum is part of your pelvis.

• **Coccyx.** The last part of your backbone is the coccyx, or tailbone. Like the sacrum, this starts out as several bones when you're born, and fuses into one when you grow older.

Your spine is flexible because the vertebrae aren't fused to one another. You'd be pretty stiff if they were! Instead, discs of cartilage are between the vertebrae. This cartilage not only allows us to bend the spine, but it also cushions the spine when you're doing something active such as running or jumping.

DID YOU KNOW?

Infants have more bones in their bodies than adults. That's because some of a baby's bones are still "knitting" together, making several bones into one.

ligament: an elastic tissue that attaches bones to each other.

fracture: a break.

collagen: a protein that provides a soft framework for bone.

lamellar bone: a strong, hard type of bone material.

THE LEG BONE'S CONNECTED TO THE . . .

If your bones were fastened firmly together, you wouldn't be able to bend, twist, or move the way you do. But your bones can't just be floating around inside your skin, either. So that they can move, the bones are attached to each other by **ligaments**.

Ligaments are elastic, fibrous structures. Since they're elastic, they can stretch slightly. That's why you stretch before playing sports or exercising. You're making your body more flexible by stretching out the muscles and ligaments in preparation for action.

BREAK TIME

Imagine playing soccer when an opponent running the other way kicks for the ball, misses—and gets your leg instead. Crack! You hear a loud noise and you're on the ground, grabbing your leg in pain. The news isn't great—you've got a broken bone.

DID YOU KNOW?

About 6 million Americans suffer from at least one broken bone every year!

Although bones are strong, sometimes accidents happen and you end up with a broken bone, called a **fracture**. Any of your bones can break—from your fingers to your toes. If you've got a break, the doctor will take an X-ray to see what's broken and how badly. Not every break is the same. Bones can break in different ways.

For example, in a spiral fracture, a bone breaks in several places because it's been twisted. In an oblique fracture, the break is diagonal across the length of a bone. A transverse fracture is at a right angle to the length of a bone. And in a compound fracture, the broken bone pokes through the skin.

Your Heart's Cage

You can feel your ribs if you press on the side of your chest—the hard, bumpy bones under your skin. The pairs of ribs start at your backbone, curve around your body to protect your chest's organs, and meet in the front, at the sternum, or breastbone. This grouping of ribs is called your rib cage, and it does a great job of protecting your heart and lungs.

If a bone is broken, the doctor lines up the broken parts of the bone the right way and puts a cast around the injured body part to keep it from moving around. This way, the bones stay properly aligned and don't wiggle out of place while they are healing.

The broken bone and the tissue that's around it will bleed and then start to clot. After a couple of days, a substance called **collagen** creates a mesh of fibers. Through time, these fibers crisscross each other and weave into new bone material.

Your cast may come off
at this point, although this kind of bone
isn't as hard as your old bone.

Harder bone called **lamellar bone** eventually grows over the woven bone. Then, you're practically good as new.

Generally, the younger you are, the faster your bones heal. You can help the process along by eating foods that are high in calcium, the mineral that makes our bones hard. Those include dairy products, cabbage, and orange juice with added calcium. This kind of diet is important for keeping bones healthy and strong!

ESSENTIAL QUESTION

How do muscles help your body move?

MAKE YOUR OWN JOINTS

It's amazing how your joints come together and function the way they do. In fact, carpenters mimic the human body's joints when they assemble certain structures, such as a door hinge. Here's how to make model joints so you can see how the bones move together to help your body's mobility.

For each joint, you'll use two blocks of floral foam. Draw the joint parts onto the blocks and then cut them out with a craft file. When you're finished, assemble your joints to see how smoothly the parts go together.

❯ **For a ball-and-socket joint, cut a gentle "scoop" out of a square piece of floral foam.** This is the socket part of the joint. From another piece of foam, cut a straight piece that has a knob on the end. This is the ball that fits into the socket. You've got ball-and-socket joints on your hips and shoulders.

❯ **For a saddle joint, take two pieces of foam about the same size.** Round the top edges of each so they are the shape of a mailbox. From each, scoop out a saddle shape in the middle. Then flip one upside down, turn it 90 degrees, and let it rest inside the first saddle. This is like the joint for your thumb. Try moving the top saddle left and right, and then the bottom one left and right. You've got quite a bit of mobility in your thumb, but you can see how it stops at a certain point (as if you were doing a hitchhiker motion) because of the lip of the second saddle.

❯ **For a pivot joint, cut one piece of foam into a circle with the middle missing (like a donut),** and a second piece into a ball. Rest the circle on top of the ball. This is like a joint in your neck—it lets you rotate your head. Your ligaments, muscles, tendons, and skin stop it from spinning around out of control, though!

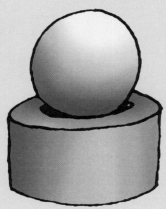

❯ **It's hard to make a hinge joint out of foam, but it's easy to spot one—just look at any door.** This is similar to your elbow or knee. You can see how it easily moves open and closed in one direction—but it cannot continue in a full, 360-degree motion.

Try this!

Can you think of a way to make your foam joints move more smoothly? Our bodies use a fluid to help. What can you use in your models?

Hip, Hip . . . Hooray?

Our hips take a lot of strain during our lifetime. Those joints move any time we move our legs, even just to sit and stand. Sometimes, they grow very painful, especially for older people, and a hip replacement is necessary. In this surgery, a doctor will remove the old hip joint and replace it with an artificial joint made from metal or plastic components.

MAKE YOUR OWN WORKING MODEL HAND

Scientists use models to better understand the concepts they are working with. Make your own hand model so you can see how the bones work together!

▶ **Trace an adult's hand onto a thin piece of craft foam.** You can do your hand if you want, but a bigger hand is easier to work with. Be sure to angle the thumb almost at a right angle to your hand. A thumb can move differently than the fingers. Cut it out.

▶ **Snip straws into ¾-inch sections.** You'll need 14 pieces altogether. Lay three pieces of straw onto one of the cutout hand's fingers, placing one for each segment of finger (between the knuckles). You don't want the pieces of straw to touch each other, so leave space right where the knuckle would be. Glue these into place.

▶ **Repeat with the remaining fingers.** For the thumb, use two straw pieces (look at your thumb to figure out where to place them).

▶ **Cut four long pieces of straw, and line them along the palm at the end of each of the fingers' straws.** Again, leave a space between the last straw segment, so it will bend. Glue these into place.

▶ **Cut five pieces of string, each long enough to run through each of the fingers,** through the palm, and give you about 4 inches leftover. Thread one string through each finger's straws, and through the thumb's straws, too. Glue (or tape) the string to the foam at the very tip of each finger. When you gently pull the strings, the fingers will move, just like in your real hand!

Think About it!

Do any other parts of your body perform the same level of precise movements as your fingers?

Chapter 5

SKIN

What keeps everything inside you from spilling out? It's your skin, of course! Your skin is the part of you that people see, it's the boundary of your physical self, and it also happens to be the largest organ in your body.

That's right—your skin is an organ, just as your heart, stomach, and liver are organs. Your skin grows with you and performs important tasks for your body. It protects you from infection and injuries, helps keep you cool or warm, and makes vitamin D.

Most of your skin is about one-tenth of an inch thick, except around areas such as your heels, where it's thicker, and below your eyes, where it's thinner. Your skin is made of two layers, the **epidermis** and the **dermis**. Let's take a closer look.

ESSENTIAL QUESTION

How does your skin differ in different parts of your body—and why?

WORDS TO KNOW

epidermis: the outer layer of the skin.

dermis: the thick layer of the skin below the epidermis.

keratin: a protein that makes up the tough part of your skin.

follicles: small cavities in the skin.

sebaceous gland: microscopic organs in the skin that secrete an oily substance.

sebum: the oily secretion of the sebaceous glands. With perspiration, it moistens and protects the skin.

ancestor: a person from your family who lived before you.

adaptation: a body part or behavior that has developed to do a specific job for an animal or plant.

EPIDERMIS

The epidermis is the water-resistant outer layer of your skin—the surface of your skin. It is a sheet made of many cells crowded together.

Think of the inside of the skin closest to the inside of you as the bottom and the outer skin as the top. New cells are always being made near the bottom of the epidermis layer. As they move upward, forcing the older cells upward as well, these cells get more and more flattened. The old cells fill with a tough protein called **keratin** and then they die, so the top part of the epidermis is made of many flat, dead, cell husks. This keratinized layer is a tough skin barrier that protects you from the outside world.

Eventually, the oldest of the dead cells—the ones on the very top layer—fall off. You lose these dead skin cells constantly, even when you're asleep. You actually lose about 40,000 skin cells every minute! But new ones are always forming and moving upward to replace them.

DERMIS

Beneath the epidermis is the dermis layer. Unlike the epidermis, the dermis is a connective tissue, meaning its cells are separated from one another by a jelly that contains lots of strong fibers. The dermis contains the skin's sweat glands, blood vessels, hair **follicles**, and nerve endings.

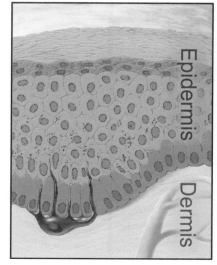

top layer

bottom layer

credit: Don Bliss (Illustrator), National Cancer Institute

Many of these nerve endings go up into the epidermis as well, so both the dermis and epidermis let you feel heat, cold, and touch.

Sweat glands are tiny tubes that begin down in your dermis and go right through to your epidermis. This is where the sweat—mostly water with a little salt—is released on the surface of your skin. Sweat reduces your body's heat and helps keep you cool.

DID YOU KNOW?

The average person's skin weighs twice as much as their brain!

Connected to your hair follicles are small glands called **sebaceous glands**. These secrete an oily substance called **sebum**. The sebum helps keep your skin supple, so it does not dry or crack. Sebum can also help to make your skin water-resistant.

Skin isn't waterproof, but it can resist water for some time, when you take a shower, for example. But when you finally come out of the pool after swimming for hours, your skin is wrinkled. That's because the sebum has washed away after lengthy exposure to water. Scientists think our bodies react this way because we're better able to grab wet objects and walk on wet surfaces when our skin is wrinkled.

It's All the Same!

Although all skin functions the same way and serves the same purpose, skin can be different colors. There are different reasons for variations in skin color, such as genes and sun exposure. But the biggest substance that affects skin color is a pigment called melanin. Melanin's purpose is to protect the skin from harmful ultraviolet rays. Depending on where your **ancestors** lived and their exposure to the sun, you have more or less melanin in your skin, and that makes your skin lighter or darker. This **adaptation** is passed on to subsequent generations.

frostbite: an injury caused by the freezing of the skin and underlying tissues.

BRRR!

When you're cold, your skin has a rough time of it. Your body needs to keep its deeper organs warm, so it sends more hot blood there, and less of it out to the skin, which gets cold.

And what's more, remember those hair follicles? Attached to each follicle is a tiny muscle. When you're cold, those muscles contract, raising the hair follicles all over your body—making goosebumps! It could be that your body is trying to raise hair to keep you warm, similar to what an animal does with its fur.

DID YOU KNOW? You also shiver in the cold. This is when your muscles begin contracting and relaxing quickly. The contracting muscles generate heat, warming you up.

Frostbite

When it is below freezing outside, the blood vessels in your fingers and toes will contract to preserve warmth. When this happens, the flow of blood to your fingers and toes is restricted. Because less blood can flow to your fingers and toes, they lose their warmth through time and freeze. When this happens, the skin can begin to discolor, turning purple or black, and blisters can occur. This is called **frostbite**. If it gets bad enough, wounds can open on your skin and you will not be able to feel them. Disease can set in and you could lose your fingers, toes, or other parts of your body.

 (PS) **Listen to an explorer from Mount Everest talk about frostbite.**

YouTube frostbite

SKIN, HEAL THYSELF

We've seen how platelets in your blood close up wounds by clotting the blood and forming scabs. But what happens if it's a more serious injury, such as a large or deep cut or a bad burn? Your skin heals these, too, although sometimes you need help from a doctor in the form of stitches. Then, it's up to your body to heal that damage to your skin.

When you have a more serious injury to your skin, scar tissue forms at the wound.

Scar tissue is a little different from normal skin. It doesn't have hair follicles or sweat glands. It also makes the skin look different from normal, so you'll see a scar even after the healing is done.

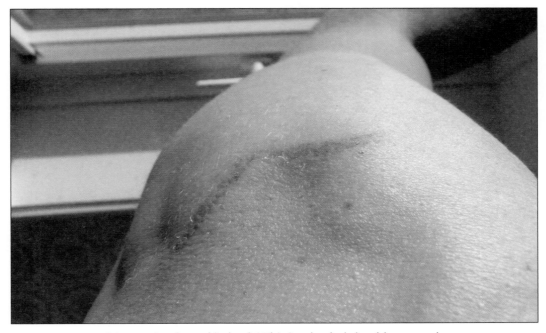

It's amazing how skin heals! This is a healed shoulder wound.

WORDS TO KNOW

friction ridges: tiny, raised portions of the skin that create fingerprints.

ultraviolet (UV): invisible radiation produced by the sun.

Scarred skin is usually thicker and paler than normal skin. It also doesn't move as easily as regular skin does. It's a little tighter. Scarred skin is also more sensitive to sunlight.

FINGERPRINTS

Take a look at the tips of your fingers. Do you see the tiny, raised ridges on them? These are called **friction ridges**. You know them as your fingerprints, and they're not only different from finger to finger, but they're also different from anyone else's. Nobody in the world has the same fingerprints you do.

Fingerprints have a long history, used both as personal identification and in criminal investigations. **This timeline follows the history of fingerprinting, starting in 1000 BCE.**

PS

softschools fingerprint timeline

Your fingerprints might all look the same to you, but they have different types of patterns in them. These patterns are called loops, whorls, and arches. For example, if one of your loops leans to the left, it's a left loop. There are also tented arches, double-loop whorls, and other variations.

Sun and the Skin

The sun is so strong that it penetrates even the thickest cloud cover. If you spend long enough outdoors, you can get sunburned even on a rainy day. Even though **ultraviolet (UV)** rays make up only a small portion of the sun's rays, they're the main cause of the sun's damage to skin. UV rays can damage skin cells—and if you've ever gotten a sunburn, that's exactly what happened. The rays actually burned you, damaging and destroying your skin cells. Even without a painful burn, if you don't protect your skin, you're setting yourself up for problems down the road. It takes about 30 years for sun damage to appear—so, if you protect your skin now, you'll be incredibly grateful when you're an adult!

HAIR

Hair follicles are the parts of your skin where hair grows. Although the first place you think of hair growing is on your head, you've got tiny hairs all over your body. In fact, you've got hair everywhere except the palms of your hands, eyelids, lips, and on the bottoms of your feet. Your body hair protects your insides from dust and bacteria. For example, your nose hair catches airborne debris and stops it from entering your lungs.

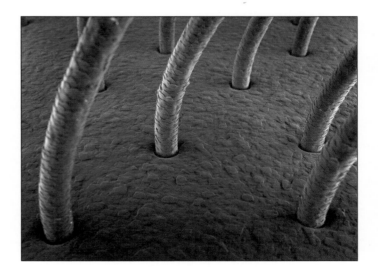

Hair is alive only at the root, where it's inside your skin.

As it grows, the cells form a protein called keratin. Then, as your hair continues to grow, the cells push out the dead cells and continue growing and pushing, growing and pushing—and your hair grows. Even though the hair on your head is made of dead cells, it can still look good because of the sebum oil that coats each strand as it grows.

It doesn't hurt to cut your hair or fingernails, but it certainly stings when you get a cut! Why? The answer to that question lies in the brain, and we'll take a look at that in the next chapter.

ESSENTIAL QUESTION

How does your skin differ in different parts of your body—and why?

NAILS

What else on your body is made of dead cells? Your fingernails! Although you may think your nails aren't as impressive as a grizzly's giant claws, your nails are pretty tough and hard, and they help protect the tips of your fingers and toes. You may not use your nails to rip apart logs or catch salmon like the grizzly, but you can use them to scratch an itch, strum a guitar, or peel an orange. Just as with your hair, the main part of the nail that you see is made of dead cells that keep getting pushed out farther as the living part of the nail grows.

Fingernails can grow pretty long if you let them, as you can see in this photo of a Chinese doctor, c. 1895–1920.

credit: Pierce, C.C. (Charles C.), 1861-1946

HOMEMADE SKIN-CARE PRODUCTS

Your skin needs to replace its moisture to stay soft and healthy. But there's no reason to rely on manufactured chemicals to do the job—you can use some natural food items instead. Here's how to make your own skin-care products to help your skin maintain its good health.

STRAWBERRY FIELD MASK

❯ **Put 1 tablespoon plain yogurt into a bowl and set it aside.**

❯ **Mash up ½ cup strawberries** with a fork and then mix them into the yogurt. (It's okay to sneak a bite or two!)

❯ **Spread the mix over your face** and let it sit for 20 minutes to deep-clean your skin. When the time's up, rinse well and pat your skin dry.

BUBBLE BATH

❯ **Carefully mix together** 1 egg white, 1 tablespoon honey, and ½ cup gentle liquid soap such as Ivory. Be careful not to be too vigorous, or else it will start foaming!

❯ **Pour the mix under running water** as you're filling the bathtub.

BATH FIZZIES

❯ **Mix together** 2 tablespoons cornstarch, 2 tablespoons citric acid powder (available at health food stores), and ¼ cup baking soda.

❯ **Add in 3 tablespoons canola oil and mix really well.** Add food coloring (optional) and essential oil (optional, to add a fragrance). You'll end up with a soft dough that feels a little crumbly.

❯ **Shape the fizzies into small balls** or press them into molds if you have them.

❯ **Let the fizzies sit for 48 hours.** When you're ready to use one, drop it into a warm bath and watch it explode into bubbles.

MAKE YOUR OWN FINGERPRINT KIT

Like a detective, you can "lift" fingerprints from around your home with this fingerprint kit. Skin has oils in it, and when you touch something, it leaves an invisible mark of your fingerprint!

❯ **Hold a graphite pencil and sandpaper over a piece of white paper.** Begin rubbing the tip of the pencil on the sandpaper vigorously. You'll start shaving down the pencil into a dust that falls onto the paper. Do not inhale any of this dust!

❯ **When you've got a good pile, pick up the paper,** roll up two sides, and pour your fingerprinting dust into a container. You're ready to hunt for fingerprints!

❯ **To test your kit, press your finger firmly and evenly on a mirror or glass** (a flat surface is ideal). Gently dip the top of a duster (such as a makeup brush) into the fingerprinting dust, and carefully brush it over the print you made. It helps to spin the brush a little bit as you move it over the print. You should be able to make out the print clearly.

❯ **Take a piece of clear tape and firmly smooth it over the print.** Then, slowly peel back the tape. You've "lifted" a print onto the tape!

❯ **Mount the tape on a white sheet of paper** and look at it closely under a magnifying glass. Look for the different patterns made by the ridges.

Fingerprint everyone in your house—let them press right on the piece of tape, dust it lightly so you can see it, and mount it on paper. Then, you'll have a record of everyone's prints!

Chapter 6

THE **BRAIN** AND **SENSES**

WOW, OUR BODIES HAVE A LOT OF STUFF TO KEEP TRACK OF!

THAT'S WHY WE HAVE A BUILT-IN CONTROL CENTER.

OUR BRAIN!

EVERYTHING YOU DO STARTS WITH AN IMPULSE IN YOUR BRAIN!

There sure are a lot of things going on in your body, aren't there? What's in charge of all this activity? Your brain! Your brain is the lead organ in your nervous system, just as your heart is the leading organ in your cardiovascular system.

Your nervous system carries messages from your brain to all the parts of your body, telling them what to do. Along with the brain, the most important part of your nervous system is your spinal cord. This nerve cord travels down through—and is protected by—the vertebrae in your spinal column. The brain and the spinal cord together are called the **central nervous system**.

ESSENTIAL QUESTION

How do your brain and senses work together?

WORDS TO KNOW

central nervous system: the brain and spinal cord.

neuron: a special cell that sends electrical and chemical messages to your brain.

axon: a fiber-like extension of a neuron that carries electrical signals to other neurons.

dendrite: a short, branched extension of a nerve cell along which impulses received from other cells are transmitted to the cell body.

cerebrum: the major part of the brain, where most higher-level functions and processing occur.

cerebellum: an area of the brain located behind the cerebrum that helps regulate posture, balance, and coordination.

brain stem: the lower part of the brain that connects to the spinal cord, responsible for basic life-support functions.

concussion: an injury to the brain caused by hitting the head very hard.

Your central nervous system contains billions of nerve cells called **neurons**. Neurons have both long arms and short arms. They look like spikey spiders. The long arms, called **axons**, send messages. The shorter ones, called **dendrites**, receive messages.

What, exactly, are these messages and how are they passed along? They are electrical signals that travel along the cell membranes of nerve cells. The fastest message, called an impulse, races along the axon. This signal then jumps along a small gap to the next nerve cell in line, and to the next, and so on.

Not all nerve cells are alike. Sensory cells have the job of carrying information to the brain from your sense organs, such as your nose or your tongue. Motor cells pass messages from your brain and spinal cord to your muscles, telling them to pick up your fork, run, or clap your hands.

DID YOU KNOW?

There are more nerve cells in one human brain than there are stars in the Milky Way!

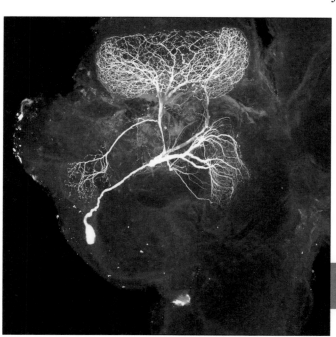

A neuron in an insect brain
credit: NICHD/N. Gupta (CC BY 2.0)

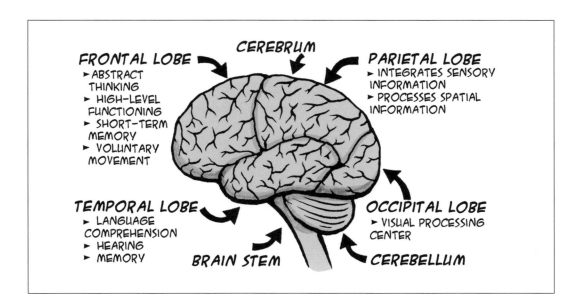

FRONTAL LOBE
► ABSTRACT THINKING
► HIGH-LEVEL FUNCTIONING
► SHORT-TERM MEMORY
► VOLUNTARY MOVEMENT

CEREBRUM

PARIETAL LOBE
► INTEGRATES SENSORY INFORMATION
► PROCESSES SPATIAL INFORMATION

TEMPORAL LOBE
► LANGUAGE COMPREHENSION
► HEARING
► MEMORY

BRAIN STEM

OCCIPITAL LOBE
► VISUAL PROCESSING CENTER

CEREBELLUM

Protect That Brain!

Our bodies are pretty tough, and, thankfully, our brains are protected by our skulls. But if someone takes a blow to the head—from a fall, a sports injury, or an accident—sometimes that makes their brain move back and forth rapidly inside their protective skull. Depending on the severity of the blow, it can sometimes cause a **concussion**, temporarily changing the way the brain normally works. Someone with a concussion might have a headache, loss of memory, or even confusion or vomiting.

CONTROL CENTRAL

The human brain has three main parts: the **cerebrum**, the **cerebellum**, and the **brain stem**. Each part manages a very important group of tasks.

The cerebrum is the biggest part of your brain and is responsible for your thinking, knowing, and remembering. It also makes you aware of everything you sense and controls your voluntary movements. The cerebrum is divided into two halves called hemispheres. The left cerebral hemisphere controls the right side of your body, and the right cerebral hemisphere controls the left side of your body. The cerebrum is also divided into sections, called lobes. Each lobe controls different functions.

The **cerebral cortex** is an important part of the cerebrum. It is the outermost layer, covering the cerebrum. Each area of the cerebral cortex controls certain **motor** or **sensory functions** in the body.

The word *cerebellum* means "little brain" in Latin. That's just what this part of your brain looks like—a small replica of your cerebrum. But your cerebellum is important for making your movements smooth and coordinated. It's what helps you walk smoothly, catch a ball, do a handstand, perform the backstroke, or even stand without falling over.

Motor and Sensory Regions of the Cerebral Cortex

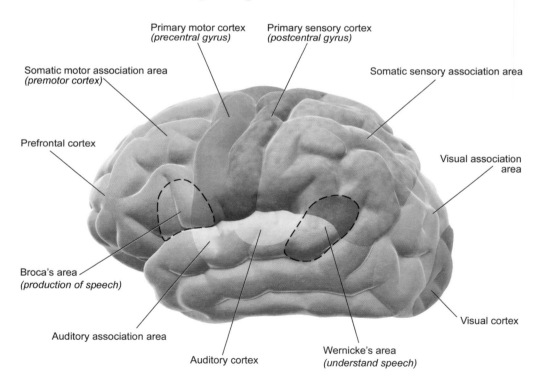

credit: Blausen.com staff (2014); "Medical gallery of Blausen Medical 2014"; WikiJournal of Medicine

The Mystery of Your Mind

Your brain is an incredible organ. In fact, scientists haven't yet unlocked many of its secrets. One of the most interesting parts of your brain can't be seen. It's your mind. What is your mind? Nobody really knows. It's impossible to define. Your brain is a physical thing, but your mind isn't. Everybody has the same general brain structure, but your mind is unlike any other mind. The mind is a combination of your thoughts, experiences, feelings, intelligence, **emotions**, memory, imagination, sense of humor—everything you are as a person. But where, exactly, is your mind? Some scientists and philosophers believe that the mind is totally separate from the brain. Others believe that without the brain, the mind cannot exist. What do you think?

Your brain stem is the smallest part of your brain and it continues downward, to the spinal cord. It's the part of your brain that controls basic life functions, such as your heartbeat, breathing, swallowing, and blood pressure. Just above the brain stem is a small part of the brain called the hypothalamus. This controls your body temperature, digestion, hunger, growth, and emotions, such as anger.

REMEMBER . . . ?

Have you ever gone into a room and then forgotten why you went in there in the first place? Or, worse, forgotten how to do math problems during a test? Your brain's cerebrum is the storage place for all your memories—bits of information that you process and save—but not all memories are the same. Short-term memory holds small amounts of information for brief amounts of time, for example, what you went into that room to do. Long-term memory holds information from more than half a minute up to a lifetime.

dementia: a group of brain diseases that cause the gradual decline in a person's ability to think and remember.

You can move information from your short-term memory to your long-term memory. For example, when you study for a spelling test or when you memorize a new friend's phone number, those memories move from short-term to long-term. It takes a conscious effort on your part to move that information between the parts of your brain responsible for memory.

Sometimes, your memory isn't forever, though. Some information is lost as you age, and some information is lost when you don't use it for a while. Do you remember last year's spelling test words? Probably not! And sometimes, memory loss is part of a condition that affects the elderly. Do you have a grandparent suffering from **dementia** who can't remember the names of their relatives or how to warm up soup?

DID YOU KNOW?

The musical genius Mozart was said to be able to play and write down all of the notes from a song he had heard only once.

People who have suffered brain injuries often struggle with basic brain and memory functions. When part of the brain gets injured, that can interrupt the functions of the brain as a whole and make day-to-day activities such as movement, retaining memories, and making new memories difficult or even impossible.

You can use your brain to relax, too. **Try meditation with the tips from this website.**

PS

🔍 NYT children meditation

BAM! DID YOU JUMP?

Sometimes, your brain or spinal cord reacts to something so fast that you don't even have time to think about it. If someone drops a pile of books in a quiet library, you jump. When someone whips a ball right at you, your hand flies up and catches it before you can think—or you duck!

That's because of something called reflexes—your brain or spinal cord fires a lightning-fast message to the part of your body that needs to respond, fast. Sometimes, your reflexes are learned, for example, when a ball comes flying at you. You've learned in the past that if you don't catch the ball or duck, you'll experience pain when it hits. You've taught your body to react very fast when it sees that ball coming.

Some reflexes you can't control, such as when the doctor taps on the tendon just below your kneecap with the little mallet. Your lower leg jerks up and forward on its own, and you couldn't stop it if you tried. That's an automatic reflex.

Your body mostly uses reflexes to protect you from injury—real or imagined.

The part of your brain responsible for memory is called the hippocampus. The structure was first noted in 1587 and later remarked as looking similar to a seahorse. **You can judge the resemblance for yourself at this website.**

PS

🔎 Kids Discover hippocampus

YOUR FIVE SENSES

Next time you go swimming, close your eyes, plug your ears, and go underwater. You'll still feel the water, but other than that, you won't be able to see, hear, smell, or taste. You've shut off four of your five main senses and lost most of your connection to the outside world. Your five senses help you keep in touch with the world you live in.

Even when you're not focusing on something, your body is still receiving input. Maybe you feel the pressure of the couch against your body, hear a dog barking outside in the distance, and smell the loaf of banana bread your dad is pulling out of the oven. Those are your senses at work, processing input from all around you.

DID YOU KNOW? Seasickness occurs when your body becomes disoriented by the constant movement around you. Your eyes can't focus on one thing and your balance is thrown off. As a result, you feel confused and sick.

What senses is this person using in this picture?

**When you focus on something,
such as when you read a book, listen to music,
or taste a soup you've never tried before,
you're consciously using your senses, too.**

But you've got more senses than you think. Beyond smelling, hearing, tasting, feeling, and seeing, you've got the senses of pain, balance, and temperature. All of these are ways your body's sense organs receive information from the outside world and relay it to your brain.

Sensing the world can be enjoyable, such as when you taste ice cream, but it can also be critical to your safety or even your life. If you see a ball flying right at your head, you can get out of the way (fast!). Or, if you hear a car coming up the road behind you while you're on your bike, you can move over farther on the shoulder of the road. Without your senses, you'd be at great risk of injury.

Your sense organs receive a message—you see the ball or hear the car—and they convert that information into the tiny electrical charges that travel along sensory nerves to the brain. Your brain sorts out the information and interprets it, so you can respond accordingly.

Upside Down

In an experiment conducted in 1896 by Dr. George Stratton (1865–1957), several participants wore glasses that inverted what they looked at, so everything looked upside down. After several days of wearing the glasses, their vision began to look normal as their eyes and brains accepted this strange flip-flop. However, when they took the glasses back off—their vision was again inverted!

You can watch a more recent version of the experiment at this website. Do you think you would be able to adjust?

🔍 BBC upside down goggles

WORDS TO KNOW

iris: a part of the eye with a muscle that is seen as a ring of color.

pupil: the dark center in the middle of your eye that changes size to control how much light enters.

retina: the part of the eye that sends images of things you see to the brain.

rod: a rod-shaped cell in the retina that is sensitive to low light. It cannot pick up colors.

cone: a cone-shaped cell in the retina that is sensitive to bright light and color.

optical illusion: a trick of the eyes that makes people see something differently than it really is.

SEEING IS BELIEVING

Your eyes are like ping-pong balls that rest in the sockets formed by your skull. They're not hollow like ping-pong balls, though. They're filled with a squishy gel that helps them hold their shape. Muscles hold your eyes in place and help you roll them around in their sockets, so you can look right, left, up, down, and cross-eyed.

The **iris** gives your eye its color and the **pupil** is the little black center of the eye. Your pupil lets in the light that you need to see. Muscles pull it open wider when you're somewhere dark and you need all the light you can get to see. When you're at the beach and the sun is reflecting brightly off the sand, the muscles squeeze your pupil smaller because you don't need all that light in order to see.

Once your pupil has let the light inside your eye, it falls on a light-sensitive layer in the back of your eye called the **retina**. The retina is covered with **rods** and **cones**, the cells that send tiny electrical messages to your brain to start interpreting what you're seeing.

Roses are red, violets are blue . . . but how do you see those colors? It starts with the object in front of you. The full spectrum of light hits a banana, for example. But only the "yellow" wavelengths bounce off of it and hit your eyes. Those yellow wavelengths stimulate your cones differently than, say, red wavelengths from a rose. That resulting "yellow" signal runs from the cones along the optic nerve to the visual part of the brain, which processes the information and then returns with an answer: That's a yellow banana!

"Eye" see you!

Optical Illusions

You can trick your eyes with **optical illusions**. For example, hold your hands in front of you, with your index fingers pointing at each other. Keep them about an inch apart—don't let them touch each other! Holding them at eye level, look past them at a blank wall. You'll see a "mystery finger" with a fingernail on each end floating between your fingers!

Try this one. Take a paper towel roll and hold it up to one eye like a telescope. Then, hold your other hand, palm facing you, up against the side of the paper towel roll. Keep both eyes open. It will look as if your hand has a hole right in the middle of it!

These tricks work because your eyes are combining two images at the same time. Your brain is still seeing each image, but blending them together.

When an image enters your eye and passes through your lens, it's flipped upside down and "projected" onto the retina in the back of your eye. The message is passed through your optic nerve to your brain—and your brain figures out that it needs to flip the image "right side up" in order to understand it.

DID YOU KNOW?

Your eye muscles let you move your eyes around without moving your head. An owl has to move its entire head to look around!

WHAT'S THAT SMELL?

Your nose is part of your respiratory system, but it also lets you get a whiff of the air around you, sometimes for better or for worse! Your sense of smell can bring pleasure, as when you catch a whiff of your favorite dessert baking in the oven. But it can also alert you to dangers, such as a gas leak or smoke from a fire.

olfactory cell: a nerve cell in your nose that helps you pick up odors.

desensitize: to lose your sense of something.

umami: a savory taste that is found in fish, cured meats, and aged cheese, among other foods.

What exactly is an odor? Think about the smell of brownies.

The brownie smell is a bunch of tiny molecules that leave the brownies, float through the air, and are inhaled by your nose. Your nose contains special nerve cells called **olfactory cells**, which catch these odor molecules from the air. Then, these cells send tiny electrical messages to your brain, which decodes these messages and says, "Brownies, yum!"

Have you ever smelled something that brought back strong memories? This happens to everyone. Scientists are still exploring why. One theory is that it's because the olfactory nerve in the brain is so close to the parts of the brain that control emotions and memory.

DID YOU KNOW?

Animals, such as your dog, are able to smell far better than you can. While you smell tomato sauce cooking on the stove, your dog can smell each of the ingredients—although a dog couldn't name these ingredients! A dog's nose is packed with hundreds more smell receptors than we have.

Brownies, yum!

Can't Smell That Smell?

Ever wonder how people can be around smelly things such as garbage or rotting fish and not seem to notice? That's because they've become **desensitized** to the smell. When an odor is present for an extended time, the receptors in your nose start to ignore them. You'd have to leave the smell for a little while and return to it before you could really smell it again.

TASTE TEST

Your tongue does all the tasting. For many decades, scientists thought the human tongue could detect only five basic flavors: sweet, salty, bitter, sour, and **umami**. However, this is still being studied and tested.

Your sense of taste is closely linked to your sense of smell, which enhances taste. When you get a good whiff of hot apple pie, your brain interprets that smell as something delicious. When you put a piece in your mouth, you're combining your tongue's input with your nose's. Yum!

That's why when you've got a cold and your nose is stuffed, it's much harder to enjoy the taste of your food—you're only getting half the enjoyment.

When you eat food, your saliva starts to break it down and carries the flavors to your taste buds, which cover your tongue. Taste buds then send messages to your brain about the flavors you're eating. In addition to the basic flavors, your tongue can sense spiciness, the temperature of foods, and metallic tastes.

vibration: moving back and forth very quickly.

sound wave: an invisible vibration in the air that you perceive as sound.

ear drum: a membrane of the middle ear that vibrates in response to sound waves. Also called the tympanic membrane.

cochlea: the part of the ear where sound waves are turned into electrical signals and sent to the brain for hearing.

TOUCHY, FEELY

You have touch, or sensory, receptors, all over your body. But some parts of your body have a higher concentration of receptors than others. For example, your fingertips have sensory receptors very close together. That's why you can feel very small differences in texture with them. But on your back, the sensory receptors are farther apart. Try having someone touch your back lightly with one finger. It's hard to identify exactly where they're touching you, isn't it?

Not all sensory receptors are alike. Some receptors feel pressure, others feel heat, and others feel cold. And some receptors sense pain. They respond very quickly to a threatening stimulus. For example, if a pin pricks you, your pain receptors fire off a message to your brain, making you jerk your finger away to safety.

DID YOU KNOW?

You probably think it would be nice to be able to turn off these pain receptors. But doing that could harm or even kill you! Pain alerts you to danger. How else would you know if you were touching a burning stovetop or if you had stepped on a nail?

LISTEN TO THIS

You can't see sound, but you sure can hear it. When your parents call your name, for example, they're really sending out invisible **vibrations** called **sound waves**. These sound waves travel through the air. Your outer ears catch these vibrations and funnel them into the rest of your ear.

That's why your outer ear looks the way it does. It's shaped like a cup so that it can catch as many sound waves as possible. Try holding your hands around your ears to make an even bigger cup. Can you hear even better now? That's because you're catching more sound waves.

After your outer ear catches the sound waves, it sends them along a channel called the ear canal. The sound waves then hit your **ear drum**, a thin membrane that acts like the skin of a drum. When you hit a drum, it vibrates, doesn't it? The same thing happens to your ear drum when sound waves hit it.

The vibrations from the ear drum then hit three little bones. These tiny bones are named after their shapes—hammer (malleus), anvil (incus), and stirrup (stapes). The vibrations run through these bones in a chain reaction and continue on their way. Next stop—the **cochlea**.

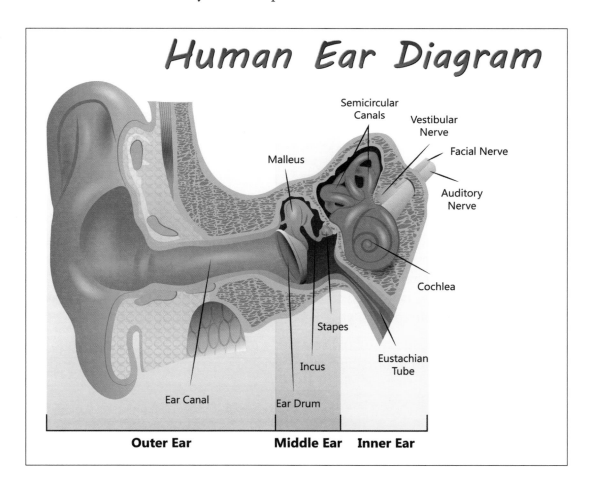

Human Ear Diagram

WORDS TO KNOW

echolocation: finding things by sending out sound waves and listening for them to bounce back.

mechanical: describing something with working parts.

The cochlea is shaped like a snail's shell. It's also filled with fluid. Here, in the fluid, the vibrations from sound waves are turned into electrical signals that are sent to your brain.

DID YOU KNOW?

A California boy who has been blind since age three taught himself to use sound to sense objects around him. He uses his tongue to make clicking sounds that bounce off objects. This technique is called **echolocation**, and it's used by dolphins and bats.

Your brain interprets the signals and then you hear your name being called!

While your senses of taste and smell use chemical reactions, your ear is all **mechanical**. It's a series of physical parts that work together, like a chain reaction, to receive sounds.

Now that we've studied several of the systems that make up the human body, we'll take a look at a system that influences all of these—the reproductive system and the genetics that make you, you!

ESSENTIAL QUESTION

How do your brain and senses work together?

Round and Round

Why do you feel dizzy when you spin around quickly? It's because your inner ear has three almost circular chambers filled with liquid. Each chamber has tiny hairs growing in it. As you move, the fluid swishes around and bends various hairs. These hairs then send messages to the brain that tell your brain exactly how you are moving your head. This is part of your sense of balance.

When you spin around, the fluid splashes crazily all over the hairs and your brain gets confusing information. It has trouble correcting your balance and you feel dizzy.

MAKE YOUR OWN INDOOR SENSORY GARDEN

Grow plants that will tickle many of your senses with this plant project.

❯ **You will need several pots with drainage holes in the bottom.** Use one pot for each kind of plant.

❯ **Put a thin layer of stones on the bottom of each pot to help with drainage.** Fill the pots with potting soil to give your plants a good home.

❯ **Choose plants or seeds from the following list to represent each of your senses.**

* Smell: mint, basil, lemon grass, or any type of herb

* Sight: colorful ivy, geraniums, any small flowering plant

* Touch: cactus, aloe, lamb's ear

* Taste: cherry tomatoes, herbs

* Sound: grasses that rustle when you blow on them

❯ **Plant your seeds and plants in the pots and water thoroughly.** Arrange your garden on a tray near a sunny window and enjoy your indoor garden with all of your senses. Don't forget to water your garden regularly!

Try This!

Can you take the idea of a sensory garden outside and plant one on a larger scale? Do some planning beforehand, researching both the plants you'd like to use and how to arrange them. Will you use pots again or design a garden to be planted directly in the soil?

TRICK YOUR EYES

In this project, your eyes will send a message to your brain and your brain will interpret that message in a way that's not really true!

❯ **For the first optical illusion, you're going to draw four rows of five colored squares.** Using a ruler, draw a 2-inch line, skip ½ an inch, and draw another 2-inch line. Do this five times. Make sure you don't move the ruler. The boxes need to be exactly the same.

❯ **Return to your first line.** Position the ruler at a right angle to the first line segment. Draw a 2-inch line down (you're starting to draw the left side of the first box). Continuing to go downward, skip ½ an inch, and then draw another 2-inch vertical line. Repeat this twice more.

❯ **Return to your first half-drawn box.** Finish this box by drawing the bottom (2 inches long) and the right side (2 inches long). Continue working your way until you've drawn all 20 boxes.

❯ **Color all the boxes exactly the same color.** When you're finished, look at the results. Do you see black (or gray) dots at the crossing points between each square? You sure didn't draw those!

What's Happening?

The sensors in your eyes are still receiving images from the colored squares and the neurons are firing, even when your eyes are looking at a blank space.

Go to this website for more optical illusions!
Do you get better at spotting the illusions the more images you look at?

🔍 optical illusions for kids

MAKE YOUR OWN MODEL EAR

You can see how your ear receives sound through fluid when you make this model ear.

❯ **Cut the bottom off an empty can using a can opener.** Pour water into a bowl and set aside.

❯ **Stretch plastic wrap over the bottom of the can.** Stretch a rubber band around the plastic wrap to keep it firmly in place.

❯ **Cut four slits in the bottom of a straw,** and then spread the tabs out a bit.

❯ **Fit a ping-pong ball against the tabs,** and tape it in place.

❯ **Securely tape the other end of the straw** to the middle of the plastic wrap on the can.

❯ **Hold the can so that the ping-pong ball is just resting on the surface of the water.** Have a friend make a noise into the air-filled can and watch the water.

DID YOU KNOW?

Even though it's only the size of a pea, the cochlea has more than 20,000 nerve cells inside it!

What's Happening?

As soon as your friend makes a noise, the sound travels through your artificial "ear drum" to the ball, where the vibrations make the ball dance on the water's surface, making ripples. This is similar to how your ear works, catching sound vibrations and passing them along to the cochlea. Test different sounds—louder and softer ones, as well as very high and very low ones. What effect do they have on the water?

Chapter 7

REPRODUCTION AND GENETICS

OUR BODIES EVEN HAVE THE ABILITY TO GROW WHOLE NEW HUMANS!

I KNOW A LITTLE ABOUT THAT!

MY MOM WAS PREGNANT LAST YEAR. NOW, I HAVE A NEW LITTLE SISTER! IT WAS SO COOL WHEN SHE CAME HOME FROM THE HOSPITAL.

SOME PEOPLE CALL IT THE MIRACLE OF LIFE. LET'S LOOK AT THE SCIENCE BEHIND IT.

The way you look, act, sound, behave, and many other things are influenced by how your biological parents look, act, sound, and behave. Can you spot similarities between yourself and your biological siblings and even cousins? Those similarities are there because of genetics.

You get the genes you have through reproduction. Half come from your mother and half come from your father. These genes—along with the environment you live in—dictate many things about you. Do you have red hair or blue eyes? What color is your skin? Genes are what decide these **traits**.

ESSENTIAL QUESTION

Why is genetics an important field of study?

SEXUAL REPRODUCTION

Life is created through **sexual reproduction**. With this type of reproduction, a new organism shares traits from each parent. The new person isn't an exact copy of either parent, but rather gets an equal number of its traits from both—and is a unique individual.

With sexual reproduction, the male and female each donate a sex cell, which join together. Once they've joined to form one special cell, the cell starts dividing into two cells, then divides again and again, until it forms what's called an **embryo**—a future human! When the embryo is a couple of months old, it's called a **fetus**.

All this happens inside the mother's body. The sex cells join in one of the two fallopian tubes that go from the mother's ovaries to the womb. The embryo and then fetus grow inside the womb, which is also called the uterus.

An embryo at 6 to 7 weeks old
credit: lunar caustic (CC BY 2.0)

Timeline of Human Development

Week 4
› the embryo looks a little like a tadpole
› a tail is visible
› heart starts beating
› neural groove forms to become the spinal cord and brain

Week 5
› ears start to form
› arms and legs that look like little buds begin to form

Week 6
› the embryo is about ¼ inch long
› two eyes form, one on each side of the head
› the brain is divided into sections, one of which is the cerebrum
› hands begin to look like flat paddles at the end of the short arms

Week 7
› the embryo is about ½ inch long
› the tail is almost gone
› lungs begin to form
› hands have fingers, but there's webbing between them

Week 8
› the formation of all organs begins
› the limbs start to grow more

Week 9
› eyelids begin to cover the eyes
› facial features develop more clearly

Weeks 10–13
› the face looks more human as the eyes are closer together
› eyelids form and are closed
› red blood cells start being produced

Weeks 14–17
› the fetus is about 6 inches long
› fine hair forms on the head
› bones become harder

Week 20
› eyebrows and eyelashes appear
› nails appear
› the mother can feel the fetus moving
› the heartbeat can be heard

Week 28
› the eyelids can open and close
› the fetus is about 15 inches long

Week 32
› body fat increases

Weeks 37–40
› the fetus is full-term and fully developed—and ready for birth!

Since the fetus can't eat or breathe on its own, it gets what it needs from the mother, receiving nutrients and oxygen from the mother's blood. Any waste products from the fetus pass through its blood and back to the mother's blood, where they're soon removed from her body along with her own waste products.

During all this, the cells of the developing fetus continue to multiply and to turn into special cells—skin cells, blood cells, nerve cells, and so on. And the fetus grows and develops. The entire process takes about 40 weeks— and then the baby is born.

DID YOU KNOW?

Another kind of reproduction is non-sexual, or asexual, which is when a new organism is produced directly off a parent organism. For example, yeast buds grow off its parent to create a new organism. In this kind of reproduction, the offspring is identical to the parent.

GOT GOOD GENES?

People are often like one or both of their biological parents in some way. Maybe you have the same eyes or hair, or the same body type, or even the same facial expressions. Maybe you share an ability to draw, to run fast, or to sing. This is because of **heredity**—the passing on of traits from parent to child. But how does it happen?

The answer lies in your cells. Each cell in your body has a chemical message that is the same in all your cells, and is unique to you as a person. The message is written in the language of genes. It's your genes that give the instructions for what color your hair or eyes are, for example.

Your genes are packed into rods called **chromosomes**. Think of each chromosome as a chapter in a cookbook. The genes are the individual recipes.

WORDS TO KNOW

dominant: a genetic trait that hides the expression of a recessive trait.

offspring: a plant's or animal's young.

recessive: a genetic trait that is hidden when a dominant trait is present.

A strand of DNA looks like a twisted ladder. Its rungs are made of four different kinds of material; adenine, thymine, cytosine, and guanine.

But what are genes and chromosomes made from, exactly? It's a substance called DNA, which is short for deoxyribonucleic acid. If you looked at DNA under a microscope, it would look like a strand.

Chromosomes, genes, and DNA are all located in the nucleus of each one of your cells. And each one of your cells has 23 pairs of chromosomes, half of which came from your mother and half from your father.

So, you really are made from equal parts of your mom and dad!

Catch That Crook!

Scientists can use DNA to catch criminals, too. Because all your cells carry your special genetic identification, any cells you leave behind at the scene of a crime will spill the beans and identify you as the culprit. If criminals leave behind a strand of hair, a broken fingernail, or even dead skin cells, scientists can pull DNA from them and find out who the bad guy is. All they need is a sample of a suspect's DNA and they can match them together.

The first case to use DNA in the conviction of a criminal was that of Colin Pitchfork (1960–), who stood accused of murder after being arrested in 1987. Along with a guilty plea, DNA collected at the crime scene and compared to that of Pitchfork's proved his guilt and helped prosecutors convict him.

DOMINANT AND RECESSIVE

In the 1800s, a scientist named Gregor Mendel (1822–1884) began studying inherited traits in pea plants. He found that when genes for a trait, such as flower color, come together from both parents, one is sometimes stronger than the other. This is called the **dominant** gene. The other gene is still there, but it won't be displayed in the **offspring**. That's the **recessive** gene.

The dominant gene usually has more influence over a trait. For example, the gene for brown eyes is dominant over that for blue or green eyes.

Many dominant and recessive traits mix and match to create unique humans. But some diseases, such as cystic fibrosis and sickle cell anemia, can also hitch a ride on recessive genes—and those can cause major problems. Scientists study genetics to help uncover some of the secrets of these serious and unwelcome gene combinations.

Genetics can be the reason you get some diseases, but other diseases are caused by bacteria that enter your body and makes you sick. We'll take a look at the system designed to fight off this kind of disease in the next chapter.

ESSENTIAL QUESTION

Why is genetics an important field of study?

Predicting Offspring

An early researcher of genetics, Reginald Punnett (1875–1967), created the Punnett square, which is still used today to determine possible outcomes for the offspring of two parents with specific traits. Take a look at this Punnett square that shows how you get blue or brown eyes.

EXTRACT SOME DNA

Ideas for supplies: rubbing alcohol, ½ cup of split green peas (or wheat germ or onions), salt, water, blender, cheesecloth, clear liquid dish detergent (not powdered or opaque), meat tenderizer that contains papain—check the ingredient list

You can't see DNA strands with your naked eye—they're 400 times thinner than human hair! But with this project, you can see "clumps" of DNA strands taken from plant cells.

❱ **About an hour before you start, put some rubbing alcohol in the freezer to get it really cold.** The colder you can keep everything in this project, the better your results will be.

❱ **Put some peas, a pinch of salt, and 1 cup cold water into a blender,** and blend on high speed for about 20 seconds.

❱ **Lay several layers of cheesecloth over an empty bowl.** Get someone to help hold it in place or use rubber bands. You can also use a rubber band to secure the cheesecloth to the blender pitcher if that's easier. Pour the mixture from the blender through the cheesecloth and into the bowl to strain it.

❱ **Squirt 2 tablespoons of dish detergent into the bowl and mix gently.** Don't let it get all foamy, so be very gentle. Mix for about 2 minutes.

❱ **Let this sit, untouched, for about 5 minutes.**

❱ **After 5 minutes, carefully fill a glass halfway with the mixture,** add a pinch of meat tenderizer, and gently stir for 15 seconds. Try not to get it too bubbly. If it gets too bubbly, very carefully blot the bubbles with a paper towel to remove them.

❱ **Get the cold rubbing alcohol from the freezer** and, pouring down the side of the glass so you don't disturb the mixture, add alcohol until the glass is just about full.

> **Let this mix sit for a couple of minutes.** A white, stringy substance will form in between the layers of soapy mixture and alcohol—that's the DNA of the peas. It's all clumped together, not in neat little strands like it is inside the cell nucleus.

> **If you shape a thin wire into a hoop or a hook, you may be able to reach between the layers and lift many strands at once.** See how long you can make them! If you'd like, look at them under the microscope. You should be able to make out little strings of DNA.

DID YOU KNOW?

Since humans first began to walk the planet, we have been attacked by viruses that can make us sick and even die. But today, 8 percent of human DNA is actually made up of the ancient viruses that used to kill us!

What's Happening?

How did you get the DNA? When you put the peas in the blender, you broke open the cells of the peas. The dish detergent released the DNA from the nucleus by breaking down the cell membranes—just like it breaks down the fatty grease on dirty dishes. The papain in the meat tenderizer is an enzyme that breaks down proteins—it releases the DNA from its surrounding proteins and then the dish soap prevents it from sticking to them again. The DNA then moves toward the alcohol, away from the soapy mixture, but it can't enter the alcohol. That's why it's found in between those two layers.

You could even extract your own DNA. Just swish a mouthful of salty water in your mouth and spit it into a cup and then follow the same directions, starting with the third step.

MAKE YOUR OWN INHERITANCE MODEL

Has anyone ever said, "You've got your grandmother's eyes!" or "Wow, you look just like your father!" If so, it's because you've had some of that genetic information passed down to you, and it's showing itself. Build this model to see how traits get passed down through time.

❯ **Start by making two basic shapes,** such as a circle and a rectangle, out of paper. These represent the parents. Set them at the top of your work surface.

❯ **Imagine that the parents had four offspring.** Make these offspring by creating four new shapes, each with one kind of circle and one kind of rectangle. You could make one very large circle with a small rectangle, or a large rectangle with a small circle. Mix these combinations any way you want. Lay your four offspring in a row right below the two parent shapes.

❯ **Imagine that two of those offspring find partners.** Select two of the offspring and give them each a partner—a new shape. One could be a triangle, and one could be a square, for example.

❯ **Set the partners next to the offspring they're paired with.** If the new pairs had offspring, what would they look like? Create offspring for both new pairs by combining the circle/rectangle combo of the original offspring with the new shape of the partners. You may have a circle/rectangle/triangle combo. Put the "second generation" offspring in a row underneath. Keep doing this, adding new shapes.

❯ **Look at the "family tree" you've created.** Do you see how certain traits could be passed down from one generation?

Think About It!

How many generations would it take to completely eliminate a particular trait?

Chapter 8

DISEASES
AND IMMUNITY

When your mom says, "Wash your hands before dinner!" you might think it's because your hands are all dirty. That may be true, but another reason to wash your hands is because germs and bacteria that other people leave behind can hitch a ride on your hands—and into your body.

Once they get into your body, they can really cause some harm by making you sick. Fortunately, your body is a strong, tough fortress. Even simple actions such as washing your hands in soapy water can prevent you from getting sick.

But what if something does enter your body, despite your good **hygiene**? How can your body fight invading germs? It all starts with your immune system.

ESSENTIAL QUESTION

How does your body protect itself from getting sick?

105

WORDS TO KNOW

hygiene: the things people do to keep their bodies and surroundings clean and in good health.

antibiotic: a medicine that can disable or kill bacteria.

phagocyte: a white blood cell that destroys invading cells.

lymphocyte: a white blood cell that remembers prior infections.

antigen: a foreign molecule on a virus or bacterium that invades your body.

This complex network of cells and organs is your defense against invading germs and bacteria that can make you sick. Different parts of your body work as a team to form your immune system. Your skin is a barrier that keeps stuff from entering your body. When you breathe through your nose, your nose hairs trap junk and keep it from entering your lungs. And your white blood cells can attack an organism that does get inside your body.

Bacteria are microorganisms that can be good or bad, depending on what kind of bacteria they are. Some bacteria are helpful to your body, such as the ones in your intestines that help break down food. Others aren't. For example, salmonella is a bacteria that can give you food poisoning and make you sick to your stomach.

Germs and bacteria can get into your body in different ways. Suppose you get a cut on your finger. If you wash it well and cover it with an **antibiotic** cream and a bandage, you make it harder for bacteria to get into your body—you've made a barrier and blocked its entry. But if you leave the cut open and don't clean or protect it, you may leave the door open for bacteria to come right in. Once they're in your body, they can jump into your bloodstream and possibly make you sick.

DID YOU KNOW?

Some animals help protect us from diseases. Opossums kill more than 95 percent of the ticks that get on them. A single opossum can kill 4,000 ticks every week, helping protect us from diseases such as Lyme disease!

In a study conducted by the Worcester Polytechnic Institute, researchers found that more than 1,300 colonies of bacteria had made their homes on 27 campus door handles alone! **See where germs live in college dorms.**

🔍 college stats bacteria

If you've got a strong immune system, though, your body can fight the infection.

Germs can also enter your body through your mouth or nose. If someone who's sick has germs on their hands and then touches a surface such as a doorknob, some of those germs are left behind. When you come along and touch the doorknob, you could pick up some of them. Germs can also travel through the air. When someone with the flu coughs, and you breathe in, the airborne germs can enter your body.

CHARGE! HOW YOUR IMMUNE SYSTEM GOES TO BATTLE

If something foreign to your body enters it, such as bad bacteria, your immune system kicks into gear, like a little army going to battle inside you. Here's how it works.

White blood cells are constantly circulating through your body. They're on patrol, keeping watch for any invading germs or bacteria. If they spot anything, they take action. One kind of white blood cell is called a **phagocyte**. The phagocytes gobble up invading organisms by wrapping themselves around the offending cells and destroying them.

Lymphocytes are another kind of white blood cell. These cells remember **antigens** that invaded your body in the past, and help destroy them if they come back. When an

Watch these white blood cells go to work attacking bacteria and protecting your body from disease!

PS

ρ white blood cells attacking bacteria

antigen enters your body, your lymphocytes find it and identify it. Then, the lymphocytes produce antibodies, which are special molecules that are made into a unique shape. Their shape lets them lock on to the antigens, like two puzzle pieces coming together.

Once the antibodies are locked into place, special kinds of lymphocytes called **T cells** come to destroy the antigens. Phagocytes are also called into action, eating up the invaders.

After the invading cells are destroyed, you're healthy again. But your immune system doesn't just wait around for another invasion. Those antibodies stay in your system, on guard. If the same type of antigens try to invade again, the antibodies and T cells remember them and prevent another infection. That's called immunity.

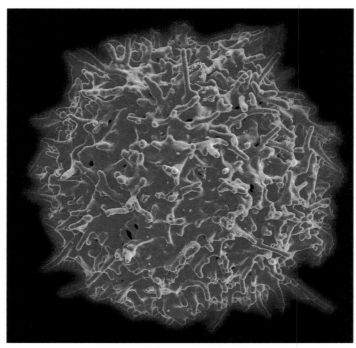

A healthy human T cell
credit: NIAID (CC BY 2.0)

What is Cancer?

You probably know cancer is a scary disease. But what is it? Cancer is a group of abnormal cells that grow together and can spread very fast. These groups of cancer cells can destroy normal cells and affect the body's ability to function properly. Doctors aren't really sure what causes some cancers, but they're working very hard to find cures and preventions.

HEY, I DON'T FEEL SO GOOD...

Everyone gets a cold now and then. That's when a common virus infects your respiratory system and you end up with a runny nose, sore throat, and a cough. Colds go away after about a week. But other kinds of illnesses can be more serious, last longer, and make you feel terrible, too. The flu shares some of the same symptoms as a cold, but it's a more severe virus. The symptoms of a flu are chills, fever, muscle pains, and feeling weak and tired all over.

Chicken pox is a virus that causes red, itchy bumps all over your body. Some people believe that chicken pox got its name because the bumps looked like chickpeas sitting on top of the skin!

Meningitis is a very serious disease and occurs when the covering of your brain and spinal cord becomes inflamed. Symptoms are a very stiff neck, bad headache, and fever.

DID YOU KNOW?

Scientists can't agree on whether viruses are alive or not. On the one hand, they can't reproduce on their own, without a host. On the other hand, they interact with their environment and can evolve through time.

Do you know anyone who is allergic to peanuts or shellfish? Allergies are actually your immune system overreacting to an antigen. You end up with an exaggerated immune response with watery eyes, sneezing, and swelling. Sometimes the response can be so severe it produces **anaphylaxis**, which is life-threatening.

Peanuts are a common allergy in children.

GERMS SHOT DOWN

Nobody likes going to the doctor to get shots. But when you get shots called **vaccines**, you're helping build your immune system against diseases that could be deadly.

Remember how your body recognizes organisms that have invaded it in the past? That's the way vaccines work. Vaccines are viruses and bacteria that have been killed or weakened. When they enter your body, your immune system produces antibodies to fight and destroy them. After the virus or bacteria is defeated, the antibodies stay in your system and make you **immune** to that disease. That's why vaccines are also called immunizations.

Vaccinate!

What do the most common vaccines protect against?

> › Measles is an infection that gives you a rash, fever, and cough.

> › Mumps cause a swelling of your salivary glands. They also give you a fever and headache and can lead to meningitis.

> › Rubella is another serious infection that gives you a rash and swelling of your neck glands. It's also called German measles.

> › Tetanus can make your muscles spasm tightly.

> › Pertussis (sometimes called "whooping cough") makes you cough violently and uncontrollably.

> › Polio can cause **paralysis**.

> › Diphtheria affects your heart and throat.

Many people get flu vaccines every year.
credit: U.S. Air Force

Some parents choose not to have their children vaccinated, for different reasons. Some people are afraid that vaccines cause more harm than good. Others object to vaccines for religious reasons. But scientists agree that vaccination is an important part of keeping the population as a whole as healthy as possible.

> While needles can be scary, immunity against dangerous diseases is very important. **Learn about how your body uses vaccines to fight against disease in this video.**
>
> PS
>
> 🔍 NOVA immunity and vaccines

CARING FOR YOUR IMMUNE SYSTEM

Just as with all your other body systems and parts, you must take care of your immune system so it can take care of you. Fortunately, it's pretty easy to build up a strong immunity. Here's how.

Sleep. Getting enough sleep boosts your immune system, and the less sleep you get, the more likely you are to get sick.

Exercise. When you exercise, you help your white blood cells produce chemicals that are natural opponents of diseases such as cancer. You also increase the amount of white blood cells called "killer T cells." These cells seek out and destroy abnormal cells, keeping you healthy.

Eat well. Munching on natural foods such as fruits, vegetables, and whole grains (including whole wheat bread or oatmeal) keeps your entire body strong and healthy. Your immune system in particular works best when you have plenty of vitamins and minerals from super foods such as blueberries, oranges, garlic, and broccoli.

We have now finished our tour of the human body! All of the systems we've looked at work together to keep you healthy and functioning. The more you know about how these systems work, the better you'll be able to care for them for your entire life. Stay healthy!

ESSENTIAL QUESTION

How does your body protect itself from getting sick?

MAKE YOUR OWN VACCINE EFFECTIVENESS CHART

Some people don't think vaccines are necessary, while other people don't hesitate to get them. With this activity, you can find out what the data can show you.

❯ **Start by choosing a disease for which there's an existing vaccine.** A good one is measles, since most school-aged children now are required to get the measles, mumps, and rubella (MMR) vaccine before entering school.

❯ **Using a poster board, create an empty graph.** Along the bottom, measure out equal spaces and label them with dates, running from about 1950 to today. Along the vertical side, label numbers from zero to 900, and label this as "Cases in the thousands."

❯ **With an adult's permission, do some research at the library or on the internet and search for data on measles cases.** Try reputable sites such as the Centers for Disease Control and the World Health Organization. Plot the results on your chart.

❯ **When you've gathered all your data, connect the data points with one line.** What do your results show? Are there any times when the data made a big change—either lower or higher? How did the introduction of the vaccine in 1963 make an impact? If there were any dramatic increases after that, can you identify why they occurred?

Think About It!

What other vaccines can you study the impact of? Are there any diseases that seemed to have been eradicated, but have now returned? Why do you think that would be?

STAY CLEAN, STAY HEALTHY!

You know staying clean helps your body fight germs. And eating well does the same thing! Here are some homemade ways you can help your body stay healthy.

HOMEMADE SOAP

❯ Put some leftover bits of bar soap in a microwaveable bowl.

❯ Microwave the soap for about 10 seconds, until everything is warm and very soft, but not runny.

❯ Put a little squirt of liquid hand soap in your hands, then gather up a small amount of the softened soap.

❯ Squeeze the soap together into little balls. After they've hardened, you can put them in a bowl by the sink.

IMMUNITY SLUSHY DRINK

When you eat foods that are high in vitamins and minerals, you help your immune system build up the strength it needs to fight invading bacteria. Here's a recipe that's loaded with vitamin C to help keep you healthy.

❯ Put 2 tablespoons lemon juice, 1 cup crushed ice (or whole ice, if you've got a strong blender), and ¼ cup frozen apple juice concentrate in a blender.

❯ Blend until everything's mixed and the drink is slushy.

❯ Drink and stay healthy!

DID YOU KNOW?

Laughter really does help your immune system! It releases dopamine and other chemicals into your brain, which can help decrease stress, which protects your immune system. So, giggle, chuckle, and LOL!

GLOSSARY

abdominal cavity: the middle section of the body that holds organs including the stomach, liver, large intestine, and others.

adaptation: a body part or behavior that has developed to do a specific job for an animal or plant.

alveoli: the tiny air sacs in the lungs where the exchange of oxygen and carbon dioxide takes place.

anaphylaxis: a reaction to an antigen that causes life-threatening symptoms such as welts, difficulty in breathing, and shock.

ancestor: a person from your family who lived before you.

antibiotic: a medicine that can disable or kill bacteria.

antibodies: proteins that help the immune system fight infections or bacteria.

antigen: a foreign molecule on a virus or bacterium that invades your body.

aorta: the large artery carrying blood from the heart.

appendicular skeleton: arm and leg bones.

artery: a blood vessel that carries blood from the heart to the rest of the body.

atria: the chambers of the heart that receive blood from the veins.

atrophy: a decrease in size of a body part, such as a muscle.

axial skeleton: the ribs, backbone, skull, and sternum.

axon: a fiber-like extension of a neuron that carries electrical signals to other neurons.

bacteria: microorganisms found in soil, water, plants, and animals that are sometimes harmful but often helpful.

biological: related by genes.

blood pressure: the pressure of the blood against the inner walls of the blood vessels.

bloodstream: the blood moving through the body of a person or animal.

bolus: the soft blob of chewed food that you swallow.

bone marrow: spongy tissue inside some of your bones that contains stem cells.

brain stem: the lower part of the brain that connects to the spinal cord, responsible for basic life-support functions.

bronchial: involving the tubes that enter the lungs.

bronchioles: the tiny branches inside the lungs.

capillaries: tiny blood vessels that connect the smallest arteries with the smallest veins and deliver oxygen and nutrients to the body's tissues.

carbohydrates: one of the basic building blocks of nutrition and a source of energy.

carbon dioxide: the gas that's produced as a waste product by your body.

carbon monoxide: a colorless, odorless, very toxic gas that is in cigarette smoke.

cardiovascular system: the body system that includes the heart and blood vessels. Also called the circulatory system.

cartilage: stiff, flexible tissue that mostly converts to bone in adults.

cell: the basic unit or part of a living thing.

cementum: the substance covering the root of a tooth.

central nervous system: the brain and spinal cord.

cerebellum: an area of the brain located behind the cerebrum that helps regulate posture, balance, and coordination.

cerebral cortex: the outer layer of the cerebrum.

cerebrum: the major part of the brain, where most higher-level functions and processing occur.

chamber: an enclosed space. The human heart has four chambers.

chemical reaction: the process when two or more molecules interact and change.

chromosome: a rod-shaped structure in a cell nucleus that carries genes.

cilia: tiny "hairs" that line your nose and trachea.

clot: the clump of blood proteins and cells that forms over a cut to help stop the blood flow.

cochlea: the part of the ear where sound waves are turned into electrical signals and sent to the brain for hearing.

collagen: a protein that provides a soft framework for bone.

compact bone: the white, hard, outer part of a bone.

concave: curving inward.

concussion: an injury to the brain caused by hitting the head very hard.

cone: a cone-shaped cell in the retina that is sensitive to bright light and color.

contract: to squeeze or force together.

cytoplasm: the jelly-like fluid inside a cell.

dementia: a group of brain diseases that cause the gradual decline in a person's ability to think and remember.

dendrite: a short, branched extension of a nerve cell along which impulses received from other cells are transmitted to the cell body.

dentin: the hard, bony material just under the tooth's enamel.

deoxygenated: without oxygen.

deoxyribonucleic acid (DNA): the substance that carries your genetic information, the "blueprint" of who you are.

dermis: the thick layer of the skin below the epidermis.

desensitize: to lose your sense of something.

diaphragm: the muscle that separates the chest from the abdomen.

digest: to break down food that is eaten.

digestive system: the body system that breaks down food, absorbs nutrients, and filters waste.

disease: a sickness that produces specific signs or symptoms.

dominant: a genetic trait that hides the expression of a recessive trait.

ear drum: a membrane of the middle ear that vibrates in response to sound waves. Also called the tympanic membrane.

echolocation: finding things by sending out sound waves and listening for them to bounce back.

embryo: an organism at its earliest stage of development.

emotion: a strong feeling about something or someone.

enamel: the protective outer layer on teeth.

endoplasmic reticulum: a network of membranes that makes changes and transports materials through a cell.

enzyme: a substance that causes chemical reactions to occur.

epidermis: the outer layer of the skin.

epiglottis: the flap of cartilage that covers the windpipe.

epithelial cell: a type of cell found on the surfaces of the body and the organs that acts as a protective barrier.

erythrocyte: a red blood cell.

esophagus: the long tube that connects your mouth to your stomach.

extract: to take out.

fats: one of the basic building blocks of nutrition and a rich source of energy.

feces: poop.

fetus: the human or animal stage before birth.

fiber: material in food that is mostly indigestible but stimulates the intestine to peristalsis.

follicles: small cavities in the skin.

foreign: something that's not natural to your body.

fracture: a break.

friction ridges: tiny, raised portions of the skin that create fingerprints.

frostbite: an injury caused by the freezing of the skin and underlying tissues.

genes: sections of DNA that code for a particular trait, such as brown eyes and black hair.

genetics: the study of genes and heredity. Genes are basic units in our cells that carry characteristics from one generation to the next.

germs: harmful microorganisms, which are organisms that are too small to be seen with a microscope.

gland: an organ that makes and releases substances the body needs.

Golgi apparatus: a cell organelle that tags molecules for specific areas inside or outside a cell.

hemoglobin: the protein that carries oxygen in your bloodstream.

heredity: the passing of characteristics from one generation to the next.

hormone: a chemical that travels through the bloodstream to signal other cells to do their job in the body.

humors: the fluids that people used to believe were responsible for the health of the human body. These included black bile, phlegm, blood, and yellow bile.

hygiene: the things people do to keep their bodies and surroundings clean and in good health.

immune: able to resist a certain disease.

immune system: the system that protects the body against disease and infection. Includes white blood cells.

indigestible: unable to be digested.

infection: the invasion and multiplication of microorganisms, such as bacteria and viruses that are not normally present within the body, that make you sick.

iris: a part of the eye with a muscle that is seen as a ring of color.

joint: the point where two bones meet and move relative to one another.

keratin: a protein that makes up the tough part of your skin.

lamellar bone: a strong, hard type of bone material.

leukocyte: a white blood cell.

lever: a bar resting on a pivot used to lift and move objects.

ligament: an elastic tissue that attaches bones to each other.

lobe: a section or part of the lung.

lymphocyte: a white blood cell that remembers prior infections.

lysosome: a cell organelle that contains digestive enzymes that break down waste material.

mechanical: describing something with working parts.

medulla: the part of the brain connected to the spinal cord that contains the centers controlling involuntary vital functions.

melanin: a brown pigment in skin.

membrane: the outer layer. The membrane of a cell allows materials to pass in and out.

microbe: a tiny living or non-living thing. Another word for microorganism.

minerals: nutrients found in rocks and soil that keep plants and animals healthy and growing. Salt and nitrogen are two minerals.

mitochondria: organelles within a cell that produce energy.

mitosis: the process of cell division.

molecule: a group of atoms, which are the smallest particles, bound together to form matter.

motor function: the movement of muscles to perform a specific act.

mucus: slimy, sticky substance that lines the nose.

muscle memory: the way your muscles remember how to work.

myofibril: a cylinder of muscle protein made up of stacked sarcomeres. Myofibrils are the units of a muscle fiber.

neuron: a special cell that sends electrical and chemical messages to your brain.

neurotransmitters: a brain chemical that carries information throughout the brain and body.

nucleus: the part of a cell that holds your genetic information.

nutrients: substances that organisms need to live and grow.

offspring: a plant's or animal's young.

olfactory cell: a nerve cell in your nose that helps you pick up odors.

optical illusion: a trick of the eyes that makes people see something differently than it really is.

organ: a part of the body with a special function, such as the heart, lungs, brain, and skin.

organelle: a structure within a cell that has a special function.

organism: any living thing.

ossification: the process of bone formation with the help of minerals such as calcium.

oxygen: a gas in the air that animals and humans need to breathe to stay alive.

oxygenated: filled with oxygen.

paralysis: the inability to move.

parasite: an organism that feeds on and lives in another organism.

periosteum: the membrane on the outside of a bone.

peristalsis: the squeezing process of moving food through your esophagus, stomach, and intestines.

phagocyte: a white blood cell that destroys invading cells.

pharynx: the first part of your throat, right after your mouth.

plasma: the liquid part of blood.

platelets: cells that help the blood clot, which helps stop a cut from bleeding.

pollen: a fine, yellow powder produced by flowering plants. Pollen fertilizes the seeds of other plants as it gets spread around by the wind, birds, and insects.

proteins: nutrients that are essential to the growth and repair of cells in the body.

pulmonary artery: an artery that carries poorly oxygenated blood from the right ventricle of the heart to the lungs.

pupil: the dark center in the middle of your eye that changes size to control how much light enters.

recessive: a genetic trait that is hidden when a dominant trait is present.

red blood cells: cells that carry oxygen to all the cells of the body.

reflex: an involuntary and often instantaneous movement in response to a stimulus.

regulate: to control or to keep steady.

respiratory system: a system of organs that take in oxygen and expel carbon dioxide from the body. The lungs are the primary organ of the respiratory system.

retina: the part of the eye that sends images of things you see to the brain.

ribonucleic acid (RNA): genetic material that contains the code to make a certain protein.

ribosome: the protein-making factory in a cell.

rod: a rod-shaped cell in the retina that is sensitive to low light. It cannot pick up colors.

sarcomere: a segment of contracting tissue that stacks to make up the myofibrils that, in turn, make up the muscle.

sebaceous gland: microscopic organs in the skin that secrete an oily substance.

sebum: the oily secretion of the sebaceous glands. With perspiration, it moistens and protects the skin.

sedentary: not moving around much.

senses: seeing, hearing, smelling, touching, and tasting. These are ways that people and animals get information about the world around them.

sensory function: relating to sensation or the physical senses.

septum: a thick layer of muscle between the two sides of the heart that keeps blood separated.

sexual reproduction: reproduction that joins male and female cells.

sheath: a protective cover for your muscles.

sound wave: an invisible vibration in the air that you perceive as sound.

sphincter: a round muscle that opens and closes to let something pass through.

spine: the long row of bones in your back that protect your spinal cord.

stem cell: a self-renewing cell that divides to create cells with the potential to become specialized cells.

sternum: the wide, flat bone that joins your ribs together in front, also called the breastbone.

stimulus: a change in an organism's environment that causes an action, activity, or response.

symptom: the sign of a disease, such as coughing or red bumps.

tar: brown, sticky substance found in cigarettes.

T cell: a type of white blood cell.

tendon: tissue that connects muscle to bone.

thrombocyte: a platelet.

tissue: a large number of cells similar in form and function that are grouped together, such as muscle tissue or skin tissue.

trachea: your windpipe, the tube through which air enters your lungs.

traits: characteristics determined by genes, such as being left-handed or right-handed.

transfusion: the transfer of blood from one person to another.

ultraviolet (UV): invisible radiation produced by the sun.

umami: a savory taste that is found in fish, cured meats, and aged cheese, among other foods.

urea: a waste product made from cells.

ureters: tubes connecting the bladder to the kidneys.

urinary system: the organs concerned with the formation and discharge of urine.

vaccine: medicine designed to keep a person from getting a particular disease, usually given by needle.

valve: a structure that controls the passage of fluid through a tube, such as blood through veins.

vein: a blood vessel that carries blood to the heart.

vena cava: the main vein carrying blood into the heart.

ventricles: the chambers in the heart from where blood is forced into arteries.

vertebrae: the bones that make up the spinal column.

vertical: straight up and down.

vibration: moving back and forth very quickly.

villi: the thread-sized "fingers" along the surface of membranes.

virus: a non-living microbe that can cause disease. It can only spread inside the living cells of an organism.

white blood cells: cells that protect against infection by destroying diseased cells and germs.

X-ray: a photograph taken by using X-rays, a wavelength that can penetrate a solid.

Metric Conversions

Use this chart to find the metric equivalents to the English measurements in this book. If you need to know a half measurement, divide by two. If you need to know twice the measurement, multiply by two. How do you find a quarter measurement? How do you find three times the measurement?

English	Metric
1 inch	2.5 centimeters
1 foot	30.5 centimeters
1 yard	0.9 meter
1 mile	1.6 kilometers
1 pound	0.5 kilogram
1 teaspoon	5 milliliters
1 tablespoon	15 milliliters
1 cup	237 milliliters

BOOKS

Amsel, Sheri. *The Everything Kids' Human Body Book*. Simon and Schuster, 2012.

Bennett, Howard. *The Fantastic Body: What Makes You Tick & How You Get Sick*. Rodale Kids, 2017.

Columbo, Luann. *Inside Out Human Body.* becker&mayer! kids, 2017.

Daniels, Patricia, Christina Wilsdon, and Jen Agresta. *Ultimate Bodypedia*. National Geographic Kids, 2014.

DK. *Human Body!* DK Children, 2017.

National Geographic Kids. *Weird But True Human Body*. National Geographic Kids, 2017.

Wicks, Maris. *Human Body Theater: A Non-Fiction Revue*. Macmillan, 2015.

Winston, Robert. *My Amazing Body Machine*. DK Children, 2017.

WEBSITES

Britannica Kids: kids.britannica.com

Centers for Disease Control: cdc.gov/family/kids/index.htm

KidsHealth: kidshealth.org

Science Kids: sciencekids.co.nz

QR CODE GLOSSARY

page 11: *med-ed.virginia.edu/courses/cell/resources/blooddisc.htm*

page 17: *khanacademy.org/science/health-and-medicine/circulatory-system/circulatory-system-introduction/v/flow-through-the-heart*

page 19: *youtube.com/watch?v=L61Gp_d7evo*

page 20: *drjastrow.de/WAI/EM/EMZelleE.html*

page 33: *todayifoundout.com/index.php/2011/07/charles-osborne-had-the-hiccups-for-68-years-from-1922-to-1990*

page 41: *vox.com/2016/8/9/12405306/antoni-van-leeuwenhoek*

page 53: *vimeo.com/66481441*

page 70: *youtube.com/watch?v=xCKg8qPOSYg*

page 72: *softschools.com/timelines/history_of_fingerprinting_timeline/287*

page 82: *well.blogs.nytimes.com/2016/05/10/three-ways-for-children-to-try-meditation-at-home*

page 83: *kidsdiscover.com/quick-reads/meet-hippocampus-memories-go-make-sense*

page 85: *youtube.com/watch?v=-kohUpQwZt8*

page 94: *optics4kids.org/illusions*

page 106: *collegestats.org/explore/bacteria-on-campus*

page 107: *youtube.com/watch?v=GbptpDSHQEM*

page 111: *youtube.com/watch?v=IXMc15dA-vw*

ESSENTIAL QUESTIONS

Introduction: Why are all of the systems of the body important? How does our body let us do what we want and keep us alive?

Chapter 1: What job does blood play in keeping your body healthy and functioning properly?

Chapter 2: How do your lungs supply oxygen to your body?

Chapter 3: Why are some foods better for your body than others?

Chapter 4: How do muscles help your body move?

Chapter 5: How does your skin differ in different parts of your body—and why?

Chapter 6: How do your brain and senses work together?

Chapter 7: Why is genetics an important field of study?

Chapter 8: How does your body protect itself from getting sick?